Liz Mitten Ryan

*with paintings
by the author*

This book contains insights supplied to the author. It is published for general information and not as a substitute for independent verification by users when circumstances warrant. It is sold with the understanding that neither the author nor publisher is engaged in rendering any specific psychological, religious, or equine advice. The publisher and author disclaim any personal liability, either directly or indirectly, for any information presented within. Although the author and publisher have used care and diligence in the preparation, and made every effort to ensure the accuracy and completeness of information contained in this book, we assume no responsibility for errors, inaccuracies, omissions, or inconsistencies herein.

www.lizmittenryan.com   **www.onewiththeherd.com**

Photographs by: Liz Mitten Ryan, Kevin Ryan, Laurie C. Munsell, April Kendrick

Photo-graphics by Peter Ryan

Published and Promoted by:

Communications/Creativity, 800-331-8355

Distributed to the trade by:

Pathway Book Service, 800-345-6665

Produced by: PublishingWorks, Exeter, NH

ISBN-13: 978-0-918880-55-0

LCCN: 2006903039

Printed in China

First Printing, 2007

CREDITS:

One with the Herd

TO THE PEOPLE

The story we have to tell is one of peace; we are creatures
of peace. Our spirits run freely through time, witness to the history of
our species. Horse energy is powerful, magnificent, as is our form.
We are here to guide you in the ways of spirit, for this is our home.
We have no fight with you; we have been your friends through the
ages. We are not beneath you, except when we carry you on our
backs. We are happy to carry you, to that place where we will all
stand together in the sun.

—from the Herd

CONTENTS

PROLOGUE

First of all, we are a privileged herd. Living as we would, in the wild—yet being loved and doted upon—is a rare occurrence in horse-human relationships. As horses, we are respected, treated as equals; our knowledge and contribution are much sought after. It is hard for people to communicate with animals when they have preconceived ideas of what is or is not acceptable in their belief system.

The secret is to be clear, open, and absolutely truthful. If you would know us, you must believe what we tell you. Let go of your fears, and your need to dominate or use us for a purpose other than our mutual enlightenment. We are together (and this applies to all life on the physical plane), searching for the way, the truth, and the life; the clear reflection here on earth, of our home in spirit. We cannot evolve alone, or become the perfect picture, when a piece of the puzzle is missing.

Language, customs, race, species, or religion are not the important factors in true communication. With pure intent, all hearts and minds are joined. Our essence is the same, and the memory of that truth is imprinted in the smallest fabric of our being. We have only to revisit that place where all is known, all is remembered—our home together as spiritual beings. To get there is to forget everything but being. This is something horses do well, and is our gift to you.

Come and be with us without agenda, seeking only what will unfold from the interaction; seeking only oneness and truth, and trust the answers you will find there.

—Limited Edition (L.E.),
Speaking for the Herd

ONE WITH THE HERD

INTRODUCTION

This is a book about my adventures in HORSE. It is a revelation and a record of my discovery and spiritual evolution, secluded from the chatter of society, in the company of my horses, dogs, and cats. Nestled in the hills in a solar house, without radio, television, or newspapers, I have ample time to commune with my animals and the nature that surrounds me. I have time to be in their midst and to listen, to meditate, and to absorb the energy of my happy herd. I don't attempt to dominate or even to structure their comings and goings, but rather just enjoy their presence, and cultivate their wisdom.

It has been almost six years now, and like venturing into a foreign culture, I have, by way of osmosis, begun to appreciate the customs; I've learned how to communicate—to both understand and be understood. I now send and receive messages telepathically, and I'm beginning to know a whole new reality through the eyes of my herd. Riding is, more often than not, an adventure and an exploration that we both enjoy. As in all relationships, time together is an opportunity to improve our communication and solidify our bonds of trust. We are equals.

I have always recognized an irrepressible calling to commune with horses, but for years it was buried beneath the more pressing issues of profession, marriage, and motherhood. When I finally heeded the ever-present call, a seeming indulgence proved to be the vehicle that would carry me to the crystallization of my life's path.

This book is bound by the threads of poetry, art, and various entries from my journal, each a cornerstone in my place of worship, and offerings from the shining spirit of wisdom, truth, joy, freedom, abundance, and love that is the essence of us all.

Throughout the chapters you will find entries from my journal—prose or poems—interspersed throughout with my artwork. I started the journal about a year before we moved to our ranch, so it spans approximately six years of self-exploration and expression. I have placed the entries in a time line as they happened in connection with chapters in the book. The art also appears in the order in which it developed from immersion in my new environment.

" Man has dreamed a strange dream of evil, which exists only in the human mind. He must awake from this dream, and listen to the truth."

—Limited Edition (L.E.)
Speaking for the Herd

As I moved further into my understanding of horses, I was called to write a book about my experience. I found that as my level of involvement and excitement with the developing book grew, the horses' interest and enthusiasm grew as well. They knew what was unfolding, not from anything I had told them, but from the pictures and concepts we shared in our minds. I would walk out to tell Prima about an idea that was developing, and before I could get the words out, I could see she was already there. It was like she was envisioning and co-creating with me; our minds were joined; our ideas together, part of a larger vision.

The understanding that was given was that the first book would set the stage for a second one, which would be written entirely from the horses' perspectives and channeled by me. The horses were also excited about working with people through informal interactive workshops and questions directed to the horses via e-mail, which would provide material for future books.

—L.M.R.

Kelsey and Leo

EDITION WARMBLOODS
GENEOLOGY

 BORN IN 2005

* 4 ORIGINAL MARES FROM THE
  SAME SIRE (FORMAAT - DUTCH)

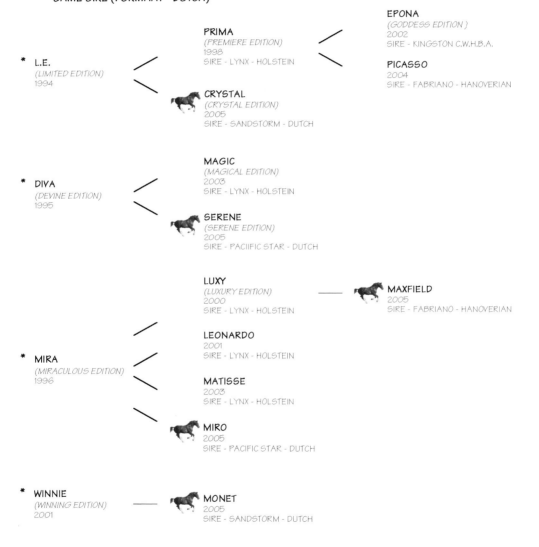

EPONA
(GODDESS EDITION)
2002
SIRE - KINGSTON C.W.H.B.A.

PRIMA
(PREMIERE EDITION)
1998
SIRE - LYNX - HOLSTEIN

PICASSO
2004
SIRE - FABRIANO - HANOVERIAN

* L.E.
  (LIMITED EDITION)
  1994

CRYSTAL
(CRYSTAL EDITION)
2005
SIRE - SANDSTORM - DUTCH

MAGIC
(MAGICAL EDITION)
2003
SIRE - LYNX - HOLSTEIN

* DIVA
  (DEVINE EDITION)
  1995

SERENE
(SERENE EDITION)
2005
SIRE - PACIIFIC STAR - DUTCH

LUXY
(LUXURY EDITION)
2000
SIRE - LYNX - HOLSTEIN

MAXFIELD
2005
SIRE - FABRIANO - HANOVERIAN

LEONARDO
2001
SIRE - LYNX - HOLSTEIN

* MIRA
  (MIRACULOUS EDITION)
  1996

MATISSE
2003
SIRE - LYNX - HOLSTEIN

MIRO
2005
SIRE - PACIFIC STAR - DUTCH

* WINNIE
  (WINNING EDITION)
  2001

MONET
2005
SIRE - SANDSTORM - DUTCH

The Horses

L.E. Limited Edition

L.E. (Limited Edition, born 1994)

Benevolent and wise, L.E. is the undisputed leader of the herd. Her two daughters are Prima (born 1998) and Crystal (born 2005). L.E. is silent and strong. She speaks only when necessary, and usually a brief glance will suffice. Revered by the herd, her decisions are well respected. She is a deep thinker and a wise elder. Always kind and respectful of people, she will nonetheless make it clear when a request is unwarranted or unnecessary. She will acquiesce with a condescending, "Oh well, I'll do it for you, you poor but kind fool, if you insist." I always defer to her judgment.

Diva (Divine Edition—10 years) and Serene

Diva (Divine Edition, born 1995)

L.E.'s full and younger sister, Diva is always ready to govern when L.E. is indisposed or out of sight. Diva's discipline is like a lightning strike to any of the lower ranks that disregard her rank or authority. She has no quarrel with others who know their place. She has even disciplined me when my affections have strayed beyond acceptability. For the most part she is quiet, orderly, second in her stall for breakfast (after L.E.), and kind to and careful of the younger ones. She is my Parelli Level 2 horse, well trained in many disciplines, and is always trustworthy when a friend asks to ride. Her bareback trot is like sitting on a cloud. Diva is mother to Magic and Serene.

Mira (Miraculous Edition—9 years) and Miro

Mira (Miraculous Edition, born 1996)

Half sister to L.E. and Diva, Mira is gentle, soft, unassuming, and sensitive. Mother to Luxy, Leo, Matisse, and Miro, she always manages to pass on her wonderful qualities to her offspring. Mira is kind and trustworthy, and the horse I usually pick to help a novice rider. Always in the background, she waits to be invited.

Prima (Premiere Edition) and Liz

Prima (Premiere Edition, born 1998)

Prima is L.E.'s firstborn foal, and mine as well. She is very much a first child, with an Alpha-type personality. But she is also a sensitive, bright spirit, gentle and kind, soft-spoken and reflective. Prima is poetic, metaphorical, and mystical. She is slow to trust, but once you have convinced her you are worthy, then she will show you the worth of her being. Prima is a light-being (highly evolved soul) with a clear purpose. She has no time for anyone who is not in their truth—by which I mean they are not yet sincerely following their intuitive and honest understanding of their unique and special life's calling. She has consequently tested and rejected a series of barn help. She does not suffer fools gladly! Her understanding, sense of humor, and quick wit are second only to her mission, which is to illuminate mankind. Prima is also and foremost my Parelli Level 2 horse. She is a joy to learn with and to ride. Her first-born is my goddess, Epona; her second is Picasso

Luxy (Luxury Edition) and Max

Luxy (Luxury Edition, born 2000)

Firstborn of Mira, Luxy is beautiful, gentle, and has always been kind and good. As a yearling she would stay and babysit her younger brother Leo, and then lead him back to Mom. As a just-started two-year-old, she would look after April, her new owner and a novice rider. Luxy had her first baby this year, and what a surprise! A big girl at 17 hands, Luxy gave birth to little Max, who was so tiny he could run through her legs. Max is darling, smart, and independent. He gallops off for trail rides with his mom and leads the other babies off on their own adventures, before galloping back to the herd.

Winnie (Winning Edition) and Monet

Winnie (Winning Edition, born 2001)

Winnie is the first to welcome guests. She is curious, friendly, and affectionate. She is also a monkey. Like the young spirit she is, Winnie can be naughty and disrespectful. She tests, but very quickly responds to clear, concise leadership. Her immediate response to discipline is, "I'm a good girl . . . I'm sorry." She is very bright and quick, but somehow also naive and innocent, like a new soul.

Epona (Goddess Edition)

Epona (Goddess Edition, born 2002)

A goddess in every way, Epona is a golden palomino who came forth from two dark bay parents. She is intuitive, all-knowing, self-assured, and independent. Even as a young foal, I could catch her eye, beckon with a raised eyebrow or crooked finger, and she would leave the herd to visit or walk with me. Epona is clear, succinct, and to the point. Always absolutely honest and direct, she will give you her opinion while still loving you unconditionally.

Leo (Leonardo, born 2002)

At 17.2 hands, Leo is Mira's second-born. With four more years to grow, he is the biggest of the Edition Warmbloods He is good-natured and well-meaning, and can blunder his way past any pecking order and be warmly welcomed by old and young alike, due to his boyish charm and innocence. Extremely intelligent, he knows what he doesn't see, doesn't exist.

Magic (Magical edition) and Epona

Magic (Magical Edition, born 2003)

Magic is guileless, soft, and sweet. She is quietly content to be a horse, and her desires are simple. She wants only to be a good mother, living among her family and friends, sleeping under the trees and the open skies. Deep, dark, and magical, she has an innate connection to horse wisdom, and a gentle way of sharing her understanding.

Matisse (born 2003)

Matisse (born 2003)

Tall, black, and drop-dead gorgeous, Matisse steals everyone's heart. He gives his heart readily as well. Warm and empathic, an old and wise soul, at age two, he fell in love with my friend Mardi, and after begging her to mount, he carried her carefully around the paddock with no tack, showing off his prize to the other horses.

Picasso (born 2004)

Picasso is the youngest of my three boys at present, although not for long, as new babies will be along in the spring. Extremely smart and athletic, Picasso follows me at the canter, stops on a dime, is graceful, balanced, and extremely self-confident. He will happily leave the herd and follow without a halter, always eager to learn something new.

Here I am with these wonderful equines, living my dream. It has taken a long time to develop and refine my vision, but after fifty-four years of looking for the perfect fit, I have left the latest fashions, the silk suits and uncomfortable footwear, for something more flattering—albeit maybe only in my own mind. My glowing youth, my energetic ambition has evaporated in the dry air of the interior grasslands, leaving a somewhat older and wiser countenance.

I have lived in the larger world of business and busy-ness, for a period running a successful fine art publishing company and commuting from our family home and studio via ferry to a downtown office in Vancouver, employing a manager and distributors for the limited-edition prints that I produced from my original art. I was comfortable at printing houses with 24-foot boardroom tables, complete with four phones and a bar sink.

A valued customer, I was often wined and dined by the executives. I was always very popular as the conversation veered toward the elusive and ethereal spiritual quest, rather than the nuts and bolts of the publishing business. I also always maintained my sense of humility, usually by committing a seriously funny right-brained act. I remember once holding a contract outlining a hefty loan from a financial backer over a candle on the dining table to get a closer look in the dimness, and watching it go up in smoke. Upon reflection, I suppose that the burned contract was a clear sign, in spite of its comic relief—a valuable indicator of what I could happily live without.

So here I am, at the moment an almost kept woman. Our decision to abandon our busy former lives, as notables on the who's-who list of our small community, has worked for me, but somehow backfired for Kevin. Architects are in hot demand in this area, including the surrounding areas of Kamloops, Vernon, and Kelowna, so Kevin now has three offices and spends a large portion of his day on the phone, and one or two days a week commuting.

Here, we are all in our truth—sincerely following our intuitive and honest understanding of our unique and special life's calling—and we expect a sincere, open, and honest reception from others. This definitely separates the invisible—no less real even though we cannot see it—from the imaginary—that which is unreal.

I flow between the worlds, but very much like Leo, what I refuse to see doesn't exist in my world. I sit at the kitchen table reading or writing, semiconscious of the goings-on in Kevin's busy day. He reads *The Guardian* weekly, while I meditate or reflect on my horses. Kevin also takes the time to meditate, walk, and commune daily, and is therefore supportive of my escape.

During the six years that we have been living what at the moment is mostly my dream, like-minded friends have materialized from the inhabitants of "Millionaires Row," located just a short drive away. Spanning the lakeshore below, the houses are segmented into 2- to 10-acre estates with architecturally diverse and impressive homes, courtesy of my busy husband.

These friends have come to our larger estate, the Gateway 2 Ranch, one of several 160- to 640-acre parcels subdivided from the original (and enormous) Stump Lake Ranch. Ten minutes from the highway, it nestles amid miles of natural grassland. One of the oldest ranches in the area borders three sides of the property, and the fourth side touches another 320-acre parcel bought by a busy lawyer who visits infrequently.

Here I breed horses, paint, and write, and Kevin practices some of his architecture from a small home office. Over the years our visitors have been witness to my unique ideas and behaviors. They often find me expounding on some new inspiration or discovery that is a direct result of my increasing connection to the natural world and to my horses, and also, my growing isolation and alienation from the real world. These visitors may be surprised by how oblivious I am to what is really happening to the rest of the globe in terms of material or physical reality.

I need very little here in terms of material things. My silk suits are covered in dust, and I am hard-pressed to find a pair of jeans and a T-shirt that are unmarred by teething horses. It is a humble existence, with just the few frills that our solar house will support. We do, however, eat well and entertain in style, sharing the mysteries of our existence with many.

Several friends have bought my horses and my paintings, and have joined in my excitement for natural horsemanship, leaving their bits and crops for halters and carrot sticks. They are also exposed to my colorful beliefs, and over time have learned to not bat an eyelash when I suggest they talk to their horses or use energy work instead of vets or doctors. Not that I don't use the medical profession; I just know when not to.

Friends come here and find solace, and a secret, which offers an immeasurable sense of joy and well-being; it seems to flow from the earth and the happy, natural state of the land and animals. Here, we are all in our truth—sincerely following our intuitive and honest understanding of our unique and special life's calling—and we expect a sincere, open, and honest reception from others. This definitely separates the invisible—no less real even though we cannot see it—from the imaginary—that which is unreal. Like the emperor's new clothes, an innocent child who didn't understand anything but truth saw through the untruth, announcing that the emperor was naked. Those who invest heavily in masquerade fall quickly away, ashamed of their exposed nakedness.

This is the greatest gift of the horses. They bring the invisible and truly meaningful realms to the surface. Their connection with the spiritual world is natural, as it is for all animals, and continued exposure to them gives us perspective and a meditative clarity that refines our expectation, and hones it to a shining finish.

I am living a dream that continues to expand beyond the boundaries of my physical self, to the greater soul of all life, where what I dream for myself is a gift for all to enjoy, and what I give to all life, I give to myself. Life is discovering itself through us.

Kevin came up with a wonderful name for it the other day: EQUINISITY—the gift of finding the unexpected and truly important perspective, through the clear and almost 360-degree vision of the equine.

Kevin came up with a wonderful name for it the other day: EQUINISITY—the gift of finding the unexpected and truly important perspective, through the clear and almost 360-degree vision of the equine.

We are all on a journey to discover our dreams, or life's dream for us. The only way we can know if the fit is right, is to try it on. How does it feel? Tight around the throat, uncomfortable in the stomach, or impossible to walk in? If your life was like mine, without enough time to shed the restrictions and reflect on a more comfortable fit, join me on a short holiday at Gateway 2 Ranch, and become one with the secrets of the herd.

One with the Herd
LIFE TODAY

I AM NOT A DISTINGUISHED RIDER; I AM A GENEROUS ONE. When I am on one of my horses—particularly the babies—every part of me is sensing their comfort or concern; it is more important than my own.

My six children and the rest of my family have always believed that the horses came first. Whether apples, carrots, horse cookies, or scratches, their every need is met with a joyful unselfishness awarded only to my adored animals. (This does not mean that my family was not equally doted on and loved as well; it's just a bit of sibling rivalry!)

My raisons d'être—numbering, at present, eleven—are my first thought upon waking in the morning. I rush to the window (we live cantilevered above and beside the barn), and there they are, waiting for their morning handouts. Living in interior British Columbia, the temperature can reach 20 below zero during the month of January. This means that I take a risk when I open the window. But regardless of Kevin's protests (he's just stoked the fire for my morning pleasure), the window must be opened long enough to throw out at least a bag of apples and carrots to the waiting throng. I call them each by name and try to aim exactly at their feet. There are, of course, the quicker con-

---

GOD IS EVERYWHERE HERE . . .

I am so filled with his presence. Today the earth sang, not softly as in spring but with great intensity and velocity. A wonderful, warm wind poured into the misty grayness that has been ours for the last month of December, filling us all with excitement, and a crazy, free feeling of joy. The horses were wild with it; manes and feet flying, they succumbed to wild abandon. Dancing, their hearts overflowed with the rightness of it all.

I drank it all in; love and admiration overflowing, expanding the shores of my being. I climbed on Prima, and the herd followed to the top of the hill, galloping down the hillside, snow flying across the valley, to their favorite place with the view of the lake.

I walked back with the dogs to a 360-degree sunset. The more I appreciated it, the more it glowed. Corals to crimsons, clouds streaking overhead, connecting the whole dome of the sky. I was so excited I shot a roll of film, and kept interrupting Kevin's business call, making faces and pointing out the window. There is no room for being sensible in the presence of such beauty!

"The ego is a transitory thing. It is here today, gone tomorrow. Those who live in spirit have no need for such a device."

—Limited Edition (L.E.)
Speaking for the Herd

tortionists who manage more than their share, and by the time everyone is satisfied, the temperature inside is 10 degrees colder, and Kevin is glaring at me.

Coffee in hand, I then take my post at the window and digest every little nuance of horse behavior for at least an hour. It is both my meditation and my breakfast.

I am suffused with joy as I tenderly watch the boys at their play. There are three at the moment: Leo, a two-year-old 17.2-hand bay, Matisse, his brother, another jumbo black, 16.2 hands as a yearling, and Picasso, a bay, only seven months old. The boys play their boy games, rearing and chasing, as the teenage girls—Winnie (three), Magic (one), and Epona (two, and my only blonde goddess among bays and blacks)—cast the occasional condescending look their way. Finally, the boys, unable to engage them any other way, walk over and politely ask permission to groom them, and the girls take it as their homage.

While all this is going on, Luxy (four) and Prima (six) take their places at the hay feeder in position next to their mothers (and everyone else's), Diva (nine), Mira (eight), and L.E. (ten).

Last to be mentioned, but the most benevolent, Queen L.E. (Limited Edition) is first in every way of the Edition Warmbloods. L.E. is the undisputed herd leader—not that she will ever resort to any form of violence to maintain her place. It is just her God-given right. She walks to her stall, and the herd parts as she glides to her position (first stall on the right), and remains there until her breakfast grain has been served. This sometimes confounds the barn help, as L.E. doesn't lift a foot until fed. (I have often had to work the manure balls between her feet with my hands if necessary, in order to clean her stall.)

The barn is always cleaned before breakfast. Some of the younger horses, always ready for a game, will wait for the wheelbarrow to be full to the brim before placing a careful foot in one corner and tipping it, to assorted reactions, depending on the mood of the shoveler.

Just as Jane and Michael Banks tested their various nannies until Mary Poppins arrived, the Edition Warmbloods have tested and tried an array of barn help. The shortest stay to date was just three weeks. Suzanna has been awarded the new title of "barn concierge," having made it to ten months at this writing. She has eyes in the back of her head to aid in her work. Prima, my six-year-old, should have been named Fearless 2 after Henry Blake's horse in **Talking to Horses**. Fearless would pick Henry up in her teeth and shake him when she was particularly excited to see him. This to me is perfectly acceptable, which is why

THE OFFERTORY

I am living in Gibsons, British Columbia, and as in A **Christmas Carol**, *I am being visited by spirits. This happens quite regularly (every other night), and I am getting concerned, and a little afraid. Are these good or bad spirits? I ask for confirmation: if they are there to help me, I will welcome them (Lord knows, I could use some help). It starts with a dream, and something is happening—like I am in a room, and someone, a face, keeps popping up at the window. They want to contact me. I am not so sure. I wake and there is a spirit inches from my face. I pull the covers over my head and hide. I ask if the spirits come from God.*

The next night I have another dream: I am on a swing, I am a child, and the music from the offertory hymn is playing in the background:

"Praise God from whom all blessings flow . . . praise God all creatures here below . . ."

I wake and the spirit is again inches from my face.

I welcome it, and it merges with mine.
I am filled with BLISS.

Diva at the lake

"You forget yourself in nature; in quiet—(true quiet void of thoughts) and you remember a truth that you knew long ago, that has drowned in the confusion of your busy life."

—*Premiere Edition (Prima)*
Speaking for the Herd

Prima rules the barn. New barn help are often put off by her pinned ears and large backside turned their way. Her aggressive posture, however, is all bluff. The remedy is to get her in a headlock and ruffle her up until, conceding, she licks, chews, and grooms her opponent, looking slightly embarrassed all the while.

How this horse came to be can only be explained by past-life issues, or maybe cellular memory (a genetic transference of learned traits). I have past-life memories of her as an Egyptian princess—she has almond eyes complete with eyeliner and shadow—and I was her handmaiden. She has not forgotten, and I am content to bask in her occasional kindness and moments of absolute trust. This becomes a tool to her credit when asked to do something too strenuous, like maintain a circle around me at liberty. She dives toward me for the join-up (which means she chooses to be with me), and buries her head between my legs. If she can't see or hear me, she is immune to my requests. I find this particularly endearing, and slip her a horse cookie or two (no one can see her chewing with her head in that position).

I know there are horse people who don't believe in food rewards, but I have found it to be a good way to solicit cooperation, like clicker training without the clicker. Eventually, I use less and less, until the reward comes at the end of an exercise. Using food rewards was the only way I could get eleven horses to follow me without halters; to jump up on things; and even to walk casually over tarps, or under flapping balloons or hula skirts—all part of my bomb proofing. Matisse will pick up a hula hoop with noisemakers in it, and drop it over Picasso's head. Picasso runs around, proud to be noticed, and then returns to Matisse, who removes the hula hoop.

This bravado has its drawbacks, however. The horses roam freely on 320 acres, and visitors crossing the property to get to our house are often surrounded and frisked. Prima once stuck her head in a car window and removed the keys. Fortunately, she didn't swallow them, and I managed to get them back.

The area we live in boasts several of the largest cattle ranches in the country, and beyond our half section, the hills and forests stretch for miles. Our neighbors are occasional cows, deer, moose, and coyotes. The land is natural grassland, dotted with lakes and forests of pine, fir, and aspen. It is a happy land, full of content creatures, and I am privileged to spend a good portion of each day in their company, wandering through this dynamic yet serene countryside.

One of my favorite pastimes is to follow the herd to the small lake at the bottom of the foal pasture. The path which they always take, one by one, winds down a slight hill through a copse of aspen and ends at a shallow lake about 3 acres in size. The horses love to bathe, splash, and munch on lake weed, belly-deep, amid the ducks and occasional muskrat, or the sandpipers and killdeer which nest there in the spring. I sit on a log by the edge, drinking in their joy and their playfulness. Such a privileged group of horses, to be able to live as in the wild, but at the same time have all of their whims devotedly met. They are loved and doted on, and they revel in it.

On a typical day the herd will generally traverse the entire 320 acres. From the lake they climb the surrounding hill to graze on assorted meadow grass and wildflowers, occasionally lifting their heads to enjoy the always expansive view. The land is an ever-changing kaleidoscope of color. There are wildflowers in spring and summer, and golden aspens in fall, set against the ever-changing skies, and framed by the distant hills and mountains. The horses spend a lot of their time at a particularly beautiful open section of meadow that overlooks a large lake, and mountains upon mountains in the distance. Whether displaying the indigo blues and amber golds of autumn, or the crystal-sparkled pastels of winter, it is a breathtaking view to the south that holds the energy of the sun, and the freshness of the changing winds. There are wild roses and thistles in the crevices, and lush bunchgrass on the plains. Here the horses graze, drink in the view, and recline contentedly among a heap of scattered, satiated figures.

There is a hill to the right, the tallest on the property. When I am looking for them, I climb it, taking a meandering walk to the grass and rock outcropping where I can study 360 degrees of lakes and woods and meadows, searching for dark and moving patches. They are usually within a short walk, and I join them, sitting on a nearby rock and absorbing the scene or offering scratches or dandelions, mingling with the herd. They are always glad to see me, and approach me with a particular area most in need of grooming, in the perfect place to receive attention. This is usually the hind end, which is always particularly itchy. There are times when I'm having a conversation with a friend while visiting the herd, and we find ourselves surrounded by looming backsides all in need of attention. Some people might find it rude, but I find it very amusing. Occasionally, the horses will say hello to me first, if the itch is not absolutely desperate, but mostly they are content in the knowledge that I accept them regardless of their manners—or lack thereof.

I think the strongest bond we share is the total absence of fear. We love and accept each other, and there is a solid trust in that relationship. There are many exciting things to explore, but I think that the anchor of the relationship is that we are learning together. I know that there is a need to guide and to educate a young horse, but I like to regard that need as flexible, and mutually rewarding. After all, we are journeying together as one in the family of spirit.

Funnel Dream

Standing in front of a funnel, which was the entrance to the world of spirit (Heaven).

God tells me I have one more thing to say, before my last breath. I am afraid, excited; this is the end of my life. I move in front of the funnel and with my last breath I say: "I love you, God," and surrender to his will.

Chapter 2

In Awe of Horses
EARLY YEARS

L ET ME GO BACK TO THE BEGINNING and tell you how I wound up in this situation, a confessed horse worshipper, living far away from most of humanity, in the comfort of my herd.

I suppose it's some kind of genetic predisposition, but from the moment I could distinguish skin from fur, I preferred the latter. I particularly remember looking at my hands and feet and thinking how strange they were; it must have been my first time in this body. Fur brought me joy, comfort: I loved most anything in fur: dogs, cats, mice, rats (although their tails bothered me).

This love ran in my family. Everyone on my mother's side was an animal nut. Surrounded by an entourage of dogs and cats, they were always ready to help any wild creature as well. My uncle built squirrel houses with the names "Sam" and "Sara" on them, and fed them crackers and peanut butter every day. My mother took this to the extreme in her later years, encouraging dozens of very large, fat, gray squirrels with 50-pound sacks of peanuts, much to the neighbor's dismay. After some time on this diet, their fur started falling out, and someone told her to quit with the peanuts because they weren't getting the variety of food they needed to be healthy. Then there was the call to the exterminator because someone had reported "roof rats." ("What are squirrels anyway?" I asked my mother—but she

IN AWE OF HORSES

Like leaves in the wind, one by one, each in its own dance, they seek the admiration of their audience. Clapping, yelping, and calling them by name. I loudly applaud, and they feed on my glee; each trying to outdo the other. I praise little Luxy for her gallop—rearing and kicking like a carousel horse she goes, and Mira, as she sails by, her neck arched and legs extended, blowing puffs of smoke out her nostrils. L.E. has all four legs six inches off the ground, and heavy horses Pearl and Millie thunder by, high-stepping with tails in the air; proud to play Warmbloods. Most of all I love to watch Diva, and I tell her how magnificent she is. Rearing, pawing at the sky, then diving and twisting, all in one motion, she darts among the others, loving my attention, and playing to the applause. Free little nature spirit; she is divine.

After all the exhilaration and release, one by one they walk quietly up to me and breathe on my face as if to say, "It's over. Did you approve of my performance? Are we still okay?" And I tell each one how wonderful and special they are to me and how honored I am to enjoy their presence.

Grandson Gabriel and the Animals

"If you were to let go of your concerns for self, for even a moment, the boundaries being just a thought would disappear. Then you would experience as we do."

—Premiere Edition (Prima)
Speaking for the Herd

never believed they could be one and the same.)

I took this love even further, as I couldn't bring myself to kill a rat. Lately we have had a pack rat twice in the top of our barn, and I thought it was cute and very smart. It would take my carrot-chopping knife, a couple of paintbrushes, and several apples and arrange them in a line. I would put them all away, only to find the same pattern laid out the next day. I bought a live trap and realized again how intelligent they were, when over and over, I found the food missing and the trap un-sprung. We finally succeeded when Kevin suggested tipping the trap slightly to increase the weight on the trigger, and leaving mounds of peanut butter, so he had to stay and lick it off. We made a procession out of relocation. My daughter, grandchildren, and I drove a few miles away to a lonely equipment shed (they like a roof over their heads), with hay for bedding, grain, apples, and other treats. Someone suggested my second pack rat could have been the first one, returning for more supplies, since the second one received the same treatment. I suppose we'll see if another one appears in the spring.

Then there were birds. I got very good at bringing them back to life with energy work, or sending them out the window with my thoughts. My most wonderful experience was when, as a child, I rescued a hummingbird that had hit the window of our summer house. My brother and I took turns holding him while he ate flowers, and we kept him comfortable until he was strong. A year after we released him, he came back and hovered by the front door to pay his respects. This may add fuel to my reputation as an eccentric, but I have held birds who were having convulsions, heads flopping on seemingly broken necks, and I have sent them such love and positive energy that an hour later, they were able to fly away. "Lazarus, go forth," I say jokingly, but it really has amazed onlookers many times.

One of my all-time favorite animals is my cat, Ben, otherwise known as Buddha, or the carpet whale. Ben doesn't spend much time in the barn, just an occasional stroll through, or he parks in one spot with his mouth open, waiting for a mouse to jump in. Ben has a huge presence, however, and a very important job at Gateway. We were at one time thinking of putting a sign at the gate that reads HOME OF BEN. Everyone, whether visitors or family, is drawn immediately to Ben. Like a huge vortex, he places himself in the center of things, and just is. Behind that innocent exterior, his job is maintaining the highest, purest, energy in the gathering.

I will have guests for dinner, and of course, Ben will occupy one of the chairs at the table. If there are not enough, he will just take one, and if someone is rude enough to dislodge him, he simply returns to his place again and

Our Cat Ben

"Think of me when you are alive in the moment; each moment is a gift

that we can only know when we are present to enjoy it"

—Min Buddha Ben (Ben)

again at every opportunity. His preferred spot is right in the middle of the table, and he will take that in a second if there is no objection.

Ben thrives on adoration. Larger than Garfield, he is a fluffy, cream-colored cloud with slightly crossed blue eyes and a soundless meow. He simply opens his mouth in agreement. Anyone seeing Ben is bowled over by his sheer bulk and his arresting demeanor. We have often thought of propping him in a chair with a beer can in his paw, and making our fortune in greeting cards, but that would be beneath his calling.

Ben, like the Buddha he is, brings out the best in everyone. He is completely disarming. Many a dog has come at him with very bad thoughts, but Ben just drops into carpet-whale position and calmly looks through them. At this point they walk away, mumbling to themselves and pretending no one saw that silly charge they made. Ben is a master at influencing reality with his thoughts, and I have learned a lot from him.

Ben is the one animal who, as far as Kevin is concerned, can do no wrong. Kevin has a healthy jealousy directed at the others from time to time, which I have been told he has for good reason. Long suffering, he has lost years of sleep to rotating whippets, who flip from side to side, stretching their bony little legs and poking you with their toenails to maintain their space. Finally they resort to poison-gas attacks if all else fails. For the most part you just have to laugh (or at least I do) as Kevin recedes to a foot-wide strip of our king-size bed and pulls the covers over his head. "Love me, love my dog." I grew up with dogs, cats, and horses. I keep making the point that if it were up to me, there would be elephants and tigers with us as well, so blessings should be counted.

Our most recent pet, as of this writing, is our Leonberger (one of the largest possible dog breeds), Ra. I guess I made a serious mistake here. When my whippet Hercules (or Hercy, as I called him) was killed by coyotes, I couldn't bear the loss. After his death, Hercy and I talked about it, and I asked him to come back as a bigger version of himself, so he would be able to keep the coyotes away from his sister, Dessy. You have to be careful what you ask for, I realized, as Ra possesses every little nuance of Hercy's former self. Despite her size, she is a confirmed lap dog, and will pin you to the couch while licking you from ear to ear. She will dig guests out from under their covers (those brave enough to sleep on the couch bed downstairs) and wash their faces for them. This dog can spin, leap, and run as fast as a whippet and has a much larger, longer tail, with the same whip action, which can clear counters or tabletops, or knock down lightweights. Like most of my animals, she is not into restraints, so will dive to the furthest corner under the porch if a collar and leash are produced. Thank God she has not attempted stairs, and there is still a bit of room in our bed.

I believe animals are more closely connected to God than we are, having none of the limiting thoughts that we do. According to well-known psychic Sylvia Browne: "Animal spirits are perfection, created that way by God, and eternally staying that way . . . they exist in a state of grace, already knowing all

Ra

they need to know before they ever come here."

Of all the animals, there has always been something indefinably irresistible to me about horses. Their expressive ears and the soft velvet of their muzzles always compel me to want to rub my face and lips across them. Horses are power and gentleness, clothed in silky fur. That indefinable attraction has never left me, from the moment I first fell in love with horses; it has lived in the pit of my stomach and has run through my mind in daydreams— that thrilling mixture of excitement and pleasure that puts me in sensory over-

Welcome to our home—would you like a seat?

load. I'm simply addicted to horses.

By the time I was six years old, I had models of horses made of china, cardboard, plastic, and fabric. I padded bookshelves with cushions and blankets, and rode them until they had a nice soft trot. (This was shortly before they were retired when no longer safe to use.) My father couldn't find his belts because they were all around the necks of my stuffed horses, donkeys, elephants, and anything else with four legs. I took them for walks; I could even get a good canter going by rhythmically pulling on the belt. I could whinny and snort, and when going anywhere I would canter or trot, slapping myself on the behind when necessary. You could see the neighbors looking from their windows, slightly perplexed as to what affliction I might have.

When I wasn't a horse, I dressed in full cowboy gear (just like Roy Rogers and Gene Autry, my heroes). I had chaps, holsters, and six guns fully loaded with caps; I rode with a whole gang of cowboy friends and their

Liz at age 6

"We respect gentleness, conviction. We respect a leader who will keep us safe, who can communicate with clear intent. I like to be treated gently; to be asked rather than told."

—Leonardo (Leo)
Speaking for the Herd

imaginary horses. Outdoors we would make horses on tree branches, tying on cushions and blankets for saddles. My artistic talent had begun to surface, and I could draw, build, or model a horse out of anything. This meant scrounging materials from all corners of our house and yard, often a difficult proposition in the city.

My mother finally could not take it anymore. I'm sure out of pity (and preservation of her sanity), she arranged for me to spend some time with real horses. My riding instructor, Mrs. Mills, was everything you might imagine of a disciplined English rider. Crop in hand, she was schooled in the stiff-upper-lip, no-nonsense method of riding. My cowboy outfit had to be replaced by jodhpurs and a hard hat. I was less than three feet tall at the time, and I sat atop the biggest horse in the stable, on whom my legs ended at mid-belly. Very quickly she had me changing leads and popping over jumps. All was well until we left the confines of the ring for a lesson on the trail. In this urban location, the trail was a mud path along the roadside, edged by a deep drainage ditch that contained the deepest, most lush green grass you've ever seen. The horse noticed this right away, and in spite of pulling with all my might, he won the tug-of-war that ensued. They should have recommended scuba gear for that ride, as into the ditch I plunged; but of course, right back on I got, little half boots squeaking in the stirrups (rolled twice for the appropriate length).

Years passed, and I shoveled, groomed, and borrowed my way to rides on any horse that was offered, at any stable. At eighteen my parents felt I was finally ready, and they agreed to buy me a horse. I wanted a horse just like Trigger, the horse of my dreams, and we drove to the country and found a symmetrically perfect little Arab palomino named Chako. Chako's best attributes were his incredibly long mane and tail. (I didn't worry about the fact that he was an untrained three-year-old.) We moved him to a boarding stable close to my home.

I got lots of how-to books, and employed my father as my training assistant. My dad's only horse skill involved patting the tongue of old Joe, a horse at the boarding stable who had learned how to garner treats with this little attention-getter. Dad became my translator, and read the instruction books while I sat on my horse. True to my only experience starting horses (as I have since started dozens) Chako didn't mind that I sat on him, but he couldn't understand the concept of "forward." I thought kicking was cruel, and thus was not much of a disciplinarian. I taught him the English language instead. He understood walk, trot, canter, and "Let's go!", and on the ground, he'd gallop over when called. My parents were sure it was going to be all over for me when he would come screeching to a halt, within a hair's breadth of my face.

Chako became my best friend. We enjoyed hanging out together. I walked him along the grassy ditches so he could have a taste of what horses living in lush green meadows took for granted. He was a city horse, and this ate away at me. Every time I'd go to see him, he'd be locked in a stall. The stable owner told me the horses all took turns in the little patch of muddy grass they called a pasture, but it wasn't enough. I pined for him to enjoy the birthright of his species.

I was living in a large house in Vancouver at the time, about thirty blocks north of where Chako was boarded. Being young and crazy at the time, one of my four roommates and I decided we would move poor Chako to our large, grassy backyard. Our house was nestled in the heart of a residential area, so my friend, Anthea, drove my little sports car while I sat on the back hood with a lead line, coaxing my horse to walk and trot through the neighborhood streets. I remember one lady yelled at us while retrieving her barking dog, and Anthea yelled back that she should keep her dog under control. I was thinking at the time that this relocation might not have been such a wise decision.

We arrived at the house, where I had installed a string line around the unfenced yard, about the size of a large city lot. Someone had told me that a string at eye level would work just fine. (I wish I could remember who that someone was!) I set up camp in the backyard, and spent several nights in a sleeping bag with my horse curled up beside me. In the morning I would feed him bran flakes from our communal kitchen, and then wake my roommates with the thunder of hooves as we played tag around the yard. It was just like having my own farm, until one day I returned home to hear the story of how my horse had escaped, spending the day in the nearby community of Dunbar, visiting the shops and movie theater (he loved popcorn.)

Chako was returned by the city health inspector, who informed me that there were by-laws against keeping horses in the city. He told me it was just my bad luck that I had chosen to keep a horse, as elephants or camels had not yet been outlawed. That was when I decided Chako needed a country home, and as university loomed ahead and my resources were dwindling, I practical-

Liz and Chako

ly gave him away to a perfect situation on a family farm.

Life went on. Studies, romance, marriage, and babies dulled my yearning, but my ever-present desire was to live in the country with six children and lots of animals, including several horses dotting the view from my windows. I attempted to have ponies when my children were young, but two incorrigible and too-small-to-reform ponies left my children disinterested. Finally, during

ONE WITH THE HERD   **59**

"Chemistry" — painting by the author

"Just out of interest" — painting by the author

their teen years, two of my daughters were won over, and we got a wonderful Arab cross with the inevitable hot blood running through his veins. We named him Tao. It took years of lessons to get him to safely carry Laurie to the jumping ring, and Cara, my youngest, to the event circuit. As the girls moved on to their studies and romances, Tao took me back to the saddle, educated Kevin in beginning riding, and fanned the flames of yearning that still flickered in my heart.

My children, almost fledged, were no longer demanding as much of my time. They had exchanged horses for wheels and were outwardly mobile. My art career, which had provided ever-increasing support for the family, was booming with the popularity of limited-edition prints and wildlife art. I could afford to indulge myself and redirect that support to horses. We owned 13 acres of property, and the taxes would be lowered if we could be classified as a farm. I could breed mares and sell the babies for top dollar to appropriate owners.

I initially proposed the breeding program as a business proposition, knowing full well that given the world's insistence on financial meaning being attached to every dream, it would be an easy sell—first to my husband, and then, our children. There was considerable funneling of time and resources in the direction of horses, which in turn would affect them. However, deep in my heart, I already knew this would not be a business, but merely an acceptable cover for my long-term love. I would at last be able to indulge my intuitive need to commune with these powerful interpreters of spirit.

I approached the project with a healthy degree of fear, having never been responsible for the care or management of horses before, other than my brief stint in the backyard with Chako. I found, however, that the horses could sense my good intentions, and became patient teachers and counselors. My venture started with three mares who had been raised in a herd, on a large ranch in the interior of B.C. It turned out to be ten miles as the crow flies from what would become our Gateway property.

The mares—L.E., Diva, and Mira—were sisters, by a Dutch Warmblood sire out of Thoroughbred mothers. They had experienced very little handling, and were left to run with their herd until the age of two, when I first met them. Amazingly, they walked right over, allowed me to halter them, and followed me calmly to the trailer. This could have been the result of my conveying to them, by words and visual images, the kind of life that was about to unfold, but since I had let them choose me, I believe higher forces were at work. I remember an animal communicator telling me that horse spirits were lining up to live with me, and this certainly appeared to be the case.

But before I could really get started, trainers were needed, and vets were required for everything. Artificial insemination was the only option for breeding, because of our location and the difficulty of transporting horses. Since I lived a ferry ride away from Vancouver (where the vets lived), and since they charged by the hour from the point of leaving home, it was really a financial issue. I began breeding right away, and two babies later, there were baby checks, and shots, gelding, and occasional ailments (mostly brought on by unnecessary worry). There were farriers, feed, vitamins, and tack (although later I switched to bareback pad and halter). The bills mounted quickly.

I still couldn't bear the idea of parting with a single one of my precious horses. I already had seven by this time, including the two foals, who were not

quite ready to be sold. About two years into breeding, dreams of land and owning a bigger property began to fill my mind. My new business, Edition Warmbloods (named after limited-edition art prints), was fast sinking into a hole—one that's familiar to most people who call "horse love" a business (it is a love, and not a very good business). I had two babies, three mares, and a cou-

ple of geldings that I had purchased, who didn't really fit my program. I spent a lot of time leading the horses to patches of succulent grass, which were few and far between, and helping them pick blackberries. Our rides were along rocky trails in the forest—not exactly my idea of open hills to run across. We needed more space.

Chapter 3

God's Place
FINDING THE RANCH

Kevin and I were scheduled for a holiday. We were headed for the Nicola Valley in B.C., "the land of a thousand lakes," and somehow, in the back of our minds, the trip was also a possible exploration of a place we might want to move to sometime in the future. We were recluses, artist and architect. We loved nature, and wanting to shed the entourage of necessities that had become our habit, longed for a simpler way of life. This dream was out there somewhere on the periphery of our present thoughts.

That is, until we saw it.

We'd decided to check out a certain parcel of land during our trip. After a pleasant ascent up a gravel road in the Nicola Valley, we suddenly found ourselves transported to the English countryside. Rows of aspen, skirting open fields like hedgerows, led us toward patches of evergreen forest. Pine and fir trees covered the hillside, at the bottom of which was a brilliant blue lake. On it went—more hills and trees, and other lakes, as far as the eye could see, all shining beneath a clear blue sky that stretched forever. I knew that this land was in my blood; I recognized it, like a sign meant for me alone.

As we drove across the hill, I did in fact ask for a sign—something irrefutable, in gold letters written across my heart.

GOD'S PLACE

There is a peace here so profound,
That you can feel the heartbeat,
and breathe in unison with the
earth.

There is a song here that is
played
in the fields, and in the forests,
and within all hearts.

There is a secret here,
That is the answer to all our
searching.

Here is this place,
God's dream and ours are one.

The sign

"My God," I asked, "let me know."

I had no sooner asked this when a cloud appeared on the horizon, its edges silver with sun (the cloud with the silver lining). I turned to Kevin, who was looking at me with a you-couldn't-possibly-pull-this-off look.

I asked innocently, "Is that cloud over our property?"—meaning the property we were going to look at—"and only our property?"

"Yes," he said cautiously.

We drove on, and after entering the front gate (a barbed-wire string of cow fence at the time), two bear cubs bounded up the hill to greet us, then bounced back to their forest home. We wound our way up the grassy road to the base of a large character fir, alone in a meadow, twisting its way to the sky. We parked there, planning to camp for the night, which would give us a chance to survey the land.

As I got out of the car and looked up, the silver of the cloud spread in horizontal bands above our heads. It was a powerful sign, and I was so filled with awe that tears came to my eyes, and shivers ran up and down my body. Poor Kevin took one look at me and knew our lives were about to change. We had found it—our home. There was no question. But were we ready? In truth, it had found us, and on its own terms and time frame. Nevertheless, we were not going to make rash decisions. We decided to camp for a couple of days, and do plenty of walking and thinking; this was a big decision, after all. We still had three children to consider (although two were on the verge of heading out on their own). It was tempting, very tempting, and the more we walked and talked, the more we felt it was right.

We found our hill at the end of the day. It was July, and hot; the grass was dried to pale gold, which glowed in the evening light. It felt like the top of the world—360 degrees of view, "surround sunset" that lit the scene. A large lake spread in front of us, and mountains, hills, plains, and lakes stretched to the horizon. This was the scene I had envisioned all those years ago when dreaming of my land. Although I didn't know it yet, far below on our left lay the valley pasture that would become our horses' favorite. It was heaven, and it could be ours.

We made an offer, not knowing quite why or how (why, maybe; but how was going to be difficult), and returned to our own acreage, which now felt very small. I, of course, ran straight to the barn to tell my horses: We were moving to horse heaven! I knew they could see it as well, through me; it was definitely the place!

We listed our property, which although large and sprawling to most people, had shrunk considerably in our minds. A six-bedroom house, a guesthouse, a house for the barn help—all set

MONASTIC LIFE

. . . somewhat like living in a monastery. Days of hard labor, fence building, clearing, moving rocks, and gathering wood; I am so exhausted. I fall into bed in a heap, clothes and all (when Kevin is away). I am in love with this place, this life, Kevin, my horses, dogs . . . But still, some fear remains—like when the woodstove starts smoking and shooting flames; and when I think about making money . . . How do I function here? My books, paints, prints, are buried; there's so much to do just to stay alive . . .

Consumerism at its worst—our house in Gibsons

on 13 acres, with a barn, ring, and surrounding pastures and woods—it was ideal for a large family with horses. Nevertheless, our home was not an easy sell. It had housed six children and an assorted mix of animals over the years; understandably, it showed some wear and tear. We had quickly corrected its largest flaws, and were, of course, willing to negotiate with the perfect family.

Then one day, the strangest thing happened. We were driving home from a visit to our land, which we had christened the Gateway 2 Ranch (because it was our gateway to all the cherished possibilities about to unfold), and suddenly, I said: "I think we will sell the house in June and move by September." This was not an educated guess based on the real estate market; rather, I felt it was plain fact. This was surprising, given the fact that our house had already been on the market for eight months, and we were worried about how we would make the payments on our new ranch.

It was already June, but the very next day a couple arrived to view our property. In addition to the couple, the family consisted of one horse and two dogs. They walked around glassy-eyed, fell in love with our house, and made an immediate offer. We were stunned; sold in June, possession date set for September 18, my birthday. Never had we been so convinced that this move was meant to be. We arranged for our youngest daughter Cara to stay in the guesthouse until graduation, just four months away, and our other two children moved on with their lives—one to university, and one to work. We set about getting ready for our new life.

Kevin and I, used to life with our large family, suddenly found ourselves family-less in a wall tent on a 320-acre ranch.

September arrived rapidly, and Kevin, as the only architect in the vicinity, had several projects being built on Stump Lake Ranch, located below. An historic cattle ranch since the 1800s, Stump Lake had been sold to a developer, and consequently, a portion had been subdivided into lakefront lots and small acreages ("small" meaning 180 to 640 acres on average). Our ranch was one of these parcels, and we were sitting above several years' worth of work, for Kevin, anyway. Who knew if the builders would have enough left over to buy my art as well when their houses were completed. This was definitely fortuitous, but had its drawbacks. As a conscientious architect, Kevin had to put his clients first, and his time was stretched between clients from our old home on the Sunshine Coast, and his new ones at Stump Lake.

I was content to live in a wall tent for a while. Kevin and I had both built and enjoyed our share of forts, so in some ways, this felt like a return to childhood. Our wall tent had a wooden floor and wooden walls about four feet high, enclosed within a canvas exterior and roof. We had a woodstove, a table and two chairs, a mattress on the floor, one dresser, and a long row

THE TENT

Still living in the tent; no communication, no water; still blissfully happy.

Almost November and still sunshine. Last night, such a warm wind—like a summer night on the coast. This whole property is my house—who needs walls? We have nestled into the landscape; road winding along its curves. Barn/suite resting against a rock outcrop. We have only improved the beauty of this place. It is symbiotic; we are looking after each other. We are somehow being removed from the rest of the world, and loving it. I am wanting to get to work and it's so hard in this state; there's so much to do to get our house. I guess everything will unfold in its time. For now I am absorbing the color, the expansiveness and the incredible changing beauty.

"The Lake at the End of the Foal Pasture" — **painting by the author**

"When you spend time in our presence; you are transported to another

world; one that is timeless and connects to that distant memory that

lingers in your hearts"

—Limited Edition (L.E.)
Speaking for the Herd

of nails for hanging everything. It was all very rustic, and the child in me was excited to begin this new adventure.

Moving day came at last, and it was the best birthday present ever. The horses were as excited as I was. I had been sharing visual images and stories of

"Dark Horse" — painting by the author

our new horse heaven for months now, and when the two large trailers arrived, seven horses trotted up the ramp, anxious to begin their new life. While the haulers were stunned at the ease of the horse-moving operation, I wasn't.

We had a long drive ahead, from the coast to the interior of British Columbia. I was driving our cat Ben, the two whippets, Herc and Dessy, and Cleo, our old Rottweiler look-alike (and my devoted protector). When we all arrived, five or so hours later, I deposited Ben in his new wall tent home, and the dogs and I ran over to the house/barn site at the other end of the property. This was about three-quarters of a mile from the tent, and a route I would walk regularly for the next four months.

The trailers arrived, and seven horses, blinking in the brilliant sun, stepped gingerly out of the trailer onto land that stretched before them as far as they could see. Only perimeter fences marked our imprint on the land, and they were a long way out of sight. There were no amenities whatsoever for these pampered city horses. They were released onto land similar in size to what an average wild herd would claim as their territory.

I am sure that watching my small herd for the next four days was the clos-

In the tent

est I have come to realizing that horses are truly part of who I am—who I have wanted to be forever. They cautiously advanced to the lake, which is the one at the end of their current foal pasture. It has become their swimming hole—their wallow and their beach home. They waded in chest-deep, drinking in the cool water, and splashing like children. Everywhere was lake weed, a new delicacy, and they slurped it up while cooling off in the heat. One by one they emerged to roll on the cotton grass by the lake's edge. Soon they were stretched out evenly across the peninsula, surrounded by water on three sides, napping in the shade of a grove of aspens.

They were not in a hurry to explore their new home. I had envisioned them galloping out of their trailer and running as far as they could, but they were content to revel in every new delight. They had accepted this new life as if knowing all along that this is what they were born to be—wild horses roaming their land. They would wander up the closest hill and survey their surroundings, drinking in the view upon every rise. The dogs and I were with them except when we slept, or when completing the few chores required for living in a wall tent.

In the morning I would put coffee on the woodstove, straighten out the sleeping bag, and sweep the floor, which was about eight feet square, the only space not filled by furniture. We had a small table and two chairs for dining inside, and a fire pit and grass patio for outdoor eating. There was a spectacular view of neighboring Kullagh Lake, about 60 acres in size and stocked with 1,500 trout, we had heard.

Our one neighbor was a black bear who had happened on our cooler one day when the door was left ajar. He was very polite, eating only a barbecued chicken, a pound of butter, and some cheese, while leaving the tomato intact except for a small bite. From then on he visited almost nightly for a while, and when Kevin was off working with his clients, the dogs and I would know he was there. Cleo, my big, brave protector, would wedge herself between me on the bed and the woodstove, about a foot away, and shake violently in protest. I felt very safe in her care, but amazingly, the bear never tried to enter if the door was closed. People had told me, of course, that canvas was not much

LESSONS IN ALONENESS

Elizabeth, where are you now? Why do you think I've left you? Your aloneness is a gift—it's important. You must be alone to know me. No phone, no way out, no one to lean on. Go into the pain; don't look for anyone but me to help you out. This is forced seclusion and it will be worthwhile. Everyone must go through the fire to refine their spirit. You are alone; you are born alone, and you die alone, but you have me; you are me. As with all things, stop struggling against it. Your aloneness is time to be with me. When you stop struggling against it, you won't feel alone. You of little faith, one day you are here with me; the next, floundering again. Jump in, feel the pain; it is purification. Don't look to others to help. They are mirrors reflecting back what you need to learn, and it is you who must learn it. They cannot save you from your lessons. Remember—to have all, you have to give all . . . and I mean all; I must come first. But my dear, you are almost there. Christ went into the wilderness for forty days, and fasted, just before he was tested, and it was all given to him. You are doing fine; you are loved by the most important person to be loved by. Again, I tell you to trust and allow. You are O.K. (Of the Kingdom). GO WITHIN.

"Exuberance" — painting by the author

of a deterrent for bears, so I was glad when he finally lost interest, and I vowed never to be so careless with my food or garbage again.

Once my chores were done, I had little else to occupy my day other than preparation of meals, which were pretty simple, and walking. I walked every square foot of the property—or should I say, trotted or cantered (even though I was on foot). I very nearly found myself ready to slap my own backside as I skipped around, yelling Whoopee! every once in a while, which was as close to a whinny as I could get. I was a horse, one of the herd, and I spent a good portion of each day in their company, apprenticing in their culture.

> They had accepted this new life as if knowing all along that this is what they were born to be—wild horses roaming their land. They would wander up the closest hill and survey their surroundings, drinking in the view upon every rise.

I ingested every little nuance of the horses' lives: how and what they ate, how they played, slept, and ran; and how they interacted with each other. I saw that they noticed everything with every part of themselves. Their ears perked up long before I could see a thing. I've read that they feel vibration through their hooves, and I witnessed that amazing

ability many times. They waited, poised, ready for rapid retreat at the sign of each new intruder. Coyotes made them wary, but basically cows, deer, and other hoofed creatures commanded their greatest attention. They would watch a deer bound by and off they'd go. It seemed that they wanted to try the movement: deliriously bucking, bounding, and running nowhere in particular, usually in circles.

I came to understand that this was a show of excitement, a display of prowess, and certainly, a joie de vivre. They loved an excuse to show off to the intruder, and at the same time, to each other. There were so many times, watching these joyful, reckless creatures, that I wondered at our ability to tame them, and at their willingness to let us. What's in it for the horse? After centuries of relationship to man, primarily as beasts of burden (and yet to a small percentage of their captors, so much more), they have mainly been captured and kept against their will—broken, as the term describes, for our use.

HORSES AND THE WIND

Horses and the wind,
run wild along the ridges,
rippling and tossing—their manes
like the meadow grass.
Leaping for joy; running among
the trees;
caressing the leaves in their
passing.

Wild and carefree; a song
Playing in my soul.

Horses and the wind,
know the truth of where my spirit
longs to be.

ONE WITH THE HERD

Why do they allow it? These powerful creatures do not need to acquiesce to our will. At any moment, they could gyrate as I had witnessed, leaving all but the most skilled rodeo rider in a broken heap.

I thought about this more and more in that unstructured time we had together. I certainly wanted to start a fresh page in this clean, new landscape. I wanted to elicit the horses' friendship and willing cooperation, rather than their grudging acceptance—and I was determined to find a way to make this happen.

Granddaughter Chiara and Magic

Picasso and Magic at the playground

ONE WITH THE HERD

Chapter 2

Gateway
THE NATURAL SOLUTION

I REVIEWED ALL I HAD READ OR EVER BEEN TAUGHT about horse training. Most of what I read was based on fear of these imposing creatures, and I knew that whatever control the trainer gained through these methods was only because the horses had allowed it. Basically, the horses had two options: to give in, or to fight to the death—either theirs, or their handlers'. I had heard all the stories of horses who had fought the lip chains, reared over backwards and hit their polls, or reared over backwards and killed their riders. When driven to a bitter fight, the outcome would not be pretty.

I had also read about the few cracks of light in the dark stable of horse experience. There were those who whispered softly and did things differently, fed, I believed, by that love, that indescribable connection which was what we strived to reach. I wanted to know more about these radical new methods that seemed to be surfacing in rapid succession.

Monty Roberts made a big bang as people began to understand that horses must surely have a language we might learn. If we could learn to listen, and possibly talk out our differences, it would be a lot less painful for both horse and rider.

There were natural horsemen suddenly popping up all over,

HOLDING GOD'S HAND

I am dreaming:

I am walking with Kevin and we are holding hands. His hand is large and warm, and I feel so safe and loved. The feeling of love is actually emanating from the hand, and it is so wonderful, I want to never let it go . . .

I wake up and the hand is still in mine; yet I look over to Kevin, who is sleeping with his back to me on the far side of the bed, and realize that this hand is not his. I held the hand for another five minutes or so before it faded away.

Gateway 2

fed and watered by the enthusiasm for this new possibility. Trainers and teachers like Pat Parelli and John Lyons made horsemanship simple, with step-by-step instructions. We could explain ourselves in the horses' language and finally be heard, and we could do this fairly, within mutually understood parameters. These were enormous breakthroughs. There was much spoken of proper alignment and clear, polite aids. Can you imagine anything more barbaric than to leap on a horse like a wildcat, spurring them to run for their lives, not having any idea what is being asked of them?

It seemed so obvious when illuminated this way: the horse would line up with our weight and body position. The lighter we were, the lighter their response would be. Sally Swift and Mary Wanless worked on the simple small details that made enormous differences in communication by body position. The horse would literally go where we looked. A rider's body must be trained to respond as a dancer's in order to form a partnership with the horse. Klaus Ferdinand Hempfling spoke of dancing, and precision in body language, but also of much more: that elusive connection of spirit, that oneness formed in our communion with the equine world.

Viewing horses as therapists was another breakthrough. I gave copies of Linda Kohanov's *The Tao of Equus* to all my horse friends, hoping they would see horses as an opportunity for new insight, and shatter the dark glass of ignorance.

Truth is therapy for our souls. The truth is, we can be friends with horses. Moreover, we can learn from them. This is the therapy our long-lost souls require. The idea of dominion over our fellow creatures as dictated in Genesis has now become a moral dilemma. Are human beings really just arrogant egotists who believe that if other species are different, then they must be inferior? Clearly, I could see how far we still had to go. I realized that the obstacles of our fear and ignorance are surmountable. That long-forgotten memory of our kinship with all life lost with the dawn of civilization, had started to return. Just like my urban herd, we had only to put ourselves in a natural setting and that memory would come back to us. It was, after all, inherent in the communal force of life that coursed through our veins.

I began to rethink my training methods—everything I had been taught. One thing, I was absolutely sure of: The instruments of torture being used to force compliance were not what was making horses bend to our will. If they complied, it was simply due to their grace, or their own willingness to do so. I had witnessed my own foals when they took their first breaths, unhampered by any human interaction. They entered the world curious, gentle, accepting, and open to what was offered: friendship or fear. Foals suck human fingers as readily as their mothers' teats. They are not at all surprised by the hideous, skin-covered creatures that welcome them to the world; they don't even seem to notice the incongruity of humans next to the soft eyes and velvet muzzle

> That long-forgotten memory of our kinship with all life lost with the dawn of civilization, had started to return. Just like my urban herd, we had only to put ourselves in a natural setting and that memory would come back to us. It was, after all, inherent in the communal force of life that coursed through our veins.

Liz and Leo snuggling

that washes them carefully and guides them to the udder.

However, the differences surface soon enough, and if the relationship is not cemented at regular intervals over the first few days, suspicion seeps in, and it is very hard to regain that initial unbiased acceptance. I remember when Dr. Robert Miller first published his book on imprinting, to the sneers and snickers of the old boys club of traditional horsemen. "Nonsense!," they said— but they quickly changed their tune when the imprinted generations went to school. There were fewer problems and less fear, and the colts learned more quickly than non-imprinted colts did.

Young foals very quickly notice that there are obvious differences between us. We smell of meat instead of the welcoming fragrance of meadow grass, and our sweat is putrid in comparison to the intoxicating scent of horseflesh. We

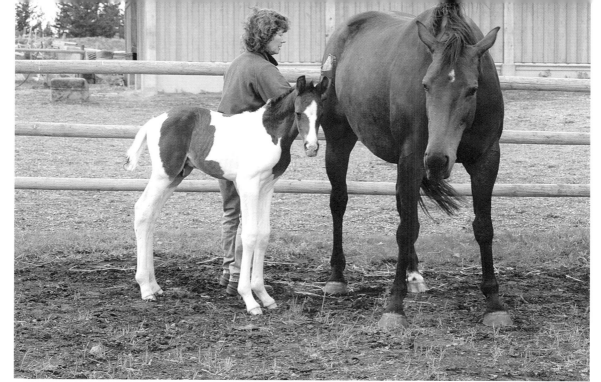

Winnie and Monet

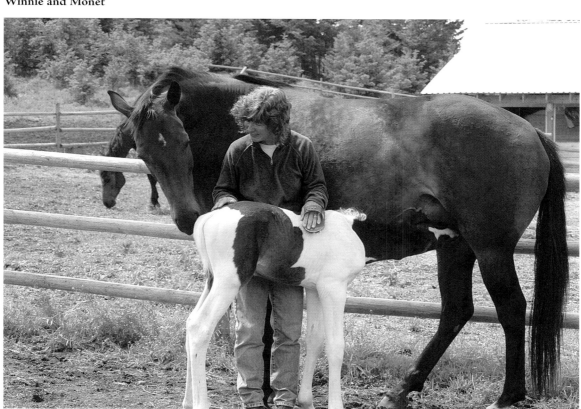

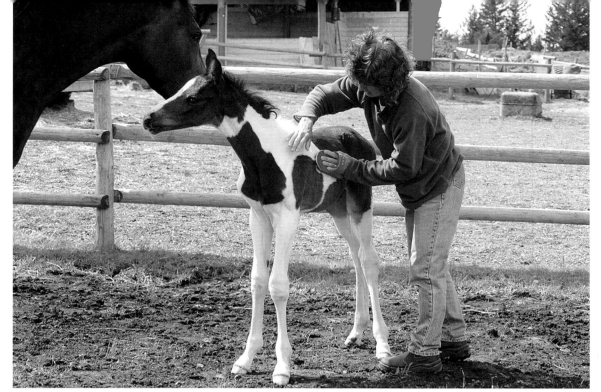

Winnie and Monet

ONE WITH THE HERD

wave strange-looking appendages and incessantly emit cacophonous sounds. In their first encounter, a foal is jolted from her peaceful reverie when a cage is put on her head and she is pulled from the safety of her mother to an insensitive encounter with one of these vile creatures. The more I immersed myself in the herd, the more my perspective morphed into one that was closer to a horse's viewpoint.

No small wonder that horses are often fearful or suspicious of our motives. What they know of us is passed down through the ages. So much of horse instinct is inherited memory. I watch as Mira's baby paws while eating his grain, just like his mother; or observe Magic, Diva's daughter, who has the same fear of stepping on things. Then there are the fears present in group memory, like water, snakes, unfamiliar objects, or being tied. Although Picasso lay on my lap and let me stroke his head regularly for the first five months of his life, he suddenly started having panic attacks when I reached for his forelock, just as his mother had done at a young age. They have both since grown past this, and his mother, Prima, now six, buries her head between my legs when needing comfort or wanting to hide.

The relationship between humans and horses is not a natural one, but in many ways, because we have to work to surmount our mutual distrust of each other, it is a gift of great value once attained. It was determined that my relationship with the horses would be just that: a gift given freely, not begrudgingly. Using information I had gained from many esteemed methods, I formulated my own system, which was based on my conviction that I should use as little paraphernalia as possible to cajole my horses into a relationship.

While I was musing on my evolving horse philosophy, September and October passed idyllically. However, by November, we'd already had the odd snow flurry, and temperatures were making the tent increasingly uncomfortable. I was having to shower at the guest ranch and it was getting downright challenging to use our outdoor toilet in the colder temperatures, particularly in the middle of the night.

Luckily, our home was slowly coming together. Situated on a hill at the top of the foal pasture, the two-story barn—a large post-and-beam structure with wooden walls and floors above—was looking very comfortable indeed. The temporary living quarters located on the upper level of the barn were secondary to the horses' needs, since we had a tent, and they had nothing at all. By

December 2, I was ready to move in, finished or not, so our furniture was unpacked and moved onto sub-floors. At last, warm and cozy, and quite appreciative of small blessings, we settled into our new home.

The horses as usual took everything in their stride, moving into the luxury of their new accommodations as if they had lived there forever. There were six large box stalls, twelve feet square, and a center aisle that was twelve feet wide. The stalls, all open, and the center aisle were bedded with a foot of sawdust. The floor had been carefully laid for drainage, starting with large rocks and working up to crushed rock, so it was dry and easy to clean. A large sawdust bin extended from the back corner of the barn to the floor above, where two large doors opened to the driveway outside for a sawdust truck to access. Next to the sawdust was the ladder to the top of the barn—and our quarters—and behind the ladder, at the end of the center aisle, was the tack and mechanical room.

We had planned for a solar house, so batteries were kept behind the tack room in an insulated space, which also doubled as a wine and root cellar. During cold weather, the tack room was heated by a propane wall heater. Wooden saddle racks lined the walls, with pegs for bridles and halters, and a big tack box sat in the corner next to some floor-to-ceiling shelves. It was the only part of the barn actually located under our living quarters, so we weren't bothered by noise—although you could definitely hear the serious banging of a cast horse, or a war going on. The stalls all had one or more feedboxes connected to the upper level by plastic tubes, and grain was stored above. I had only to climb the ladder, mix the food, and pour it down the tubes. I used a yacht braid rope that clipped in place across the stall opening for feeding, but the rest of the time the barn was open and the horses could use it as they pleased.

Generally in the morning there were snoozing horses everywhere; bodies stretched out, legs extended, and heads on their soft pillow of sawdust. Until then I'd had no idea how soundly horses slept, or that they snored. Mira's babies all snored, which was a wonderful sound! All those horses, relaxed fully, without a care in the world. This tranquil state seemed to permeate their days.

There were two large wooden hay feeders in the paddock outside, built to a height where the horses could get their heads over the top, or eat hay through slats along the sides. There was a shelf along both sides to catch their favorite crumbs of alfalfa that fell from the hay. I usually fed them a mixture of pasture grass with a bit of alfalfa. It was always available year-round to encourage the horses to return from the fields each day.

They developed a routine almost immediately, and their days had a natural cycle. They could be seen returning between six and seven each morning, head to tail usually, unless something had excited them. There were four gates out at different sides of the 10-acre foal pasture, which surrounded the inner paddock. When excited, the herd generally split—some running in the end gate, and others along the road and in the side gate. This increased their exhil-

The barn

aration, with the additional thrill of being separated, and there was always a contest to see who was the most expressive and impressive.

They would run in, leaping and bucking, do two laps of the inner paddock with the hay feeders—the paddock was 100 yards square, and had three gates—out one of the gates, around the pasture again, and in another gate. Depending on the level of excitement, this could carry on for several laps. I have never seen such beautiful movement: passage, piaffe, and canter pirouettes, all done with an elevation never witnessed under saddle, and all absolutely breathtaking. Most days they would calmly wander in, one after another, and take their places at the hay feeder, or below my window to beg for handouts.

Nowadays during the summer, I usually take my coffee and sit in the sun, back against the east wall by the door. I allow several feet of sawdust to spill forth from the front door for that purpose, and horses sprawl next to me for a morning sunbath. I grain them an hour or so after their return (when the grass is sparse), or give them a few treats, and then we have a grooming session. My horses really enjoy this free-form exercise. I pull out the brushes, shedders, scissors, and so on, and one by one, they come over for attention. They will even stand stock-still for a trim of their ears, under their chins, or their feet. They love to be looked after.

There are some who want all the grooming (Winnie, Epona, and Magic are the worst offenders), and will sidle in and place their head under the brush when I am in mid-stroke on another customer. I find this morning grooming a time when I can check not only their physical condition, but also their mental and emotional states. I always talk to my horses, telling each one how special he or she is, pointing out some wonderful attribute, such as how sweet they were to groom so-and-so, or how I enjoyed watching them leap and dive when they galloped in that day. I love each one and tell them so often. I explain what is going on in their lives, or mine, and ask for their input. I tell them how special they are to me and why. All of this takes place informally, as the interaction is on an as-needed basis.

I remember reading somewhere that you can raise the status of a herd member by grooming them in front of the herd. This also works the opposite

I love each one and tell them so often. I explain what is going on in their lives, or mine, and ask for their input. I tell them how special they are to me and why.

"Harmony" — painting by the author

way, when you embarrass a difficult horse into cooperating by making an example of them.

I remember shortly after we'd moved to Gateway, Prima went through a stage where suddenly, for no apparent reason, this imprinted two-year-old would not let me touch the top of her head. I couldn't put a halter on easily or remove burrs from her forelock. I was concerned that if she were injured, I would not be able to treat her. It was very important to be able to touch every area of the horses' bodies for this very reason. My attempts at gentle ambush while she was otherwise distracted were not working. My barn help at the time was a fellow named Lone Eagle, an English-blend native, six-foot-two and 230 pounds, a mostly gentle horseman. He was very proud of his rapport with horses. It was his idea that if we made an example of Prima in front of the herd, she would be shamed into submission. I agreed that he should try.

After breakfast one morning, he cross-tied Prima in her stall while the other horses watched. Lone Eagle stroked the "safe" areas on Prima's body, moving closer and closer to her untouchable zone. Half an hour later, we could see the other horses, who were shut in their stalls, all saying, "Come on, Prima—let him touch your head, for heaven's sake!" She gave in to peer pressure, and that was the end of the issue. After that she would give a slight pull away when approached, and then remember that no harm had come to her, and people could be trusted. Then, she actually seemed to enjoy the attention. It is interesting that some horses maintain that reserve, I suppose as a vestige of their wildness, and it has to be re-won by each new person that comes into their lives.

FOR JOY

For joy.
I watch them buck and dive and roll,
loving the earth and sky,
at home in the meadow,
belly deep in the lake,
splashing and drinking;
their bed a pillow of soft cotton grass.

One with the wind,
They wander wild and free.

Yet still they let me enter
their sacred space,
and giving me their trust;
carry me to their world

a privileged passenger,

for joy.

Chapter 5

Naked Into Truth
FINDING THE ANSWERS

THIS IS PROBABLY A GOOD TIME TO DIGRESS into some barn-help stories. Edition Warmbloods have had a colorful array to date. I am not sure whether the revolving door has to do with something the horses cook up when they don't like a person, or some character flaw that I possess and am somehow oblivious to (perhaps having to do with my missing left brain). My friends, who are varied and many, are equally puzzled. I think of myself as easygoing, open, and friendly. Some of the barn help last for weeks, while others last as long as a year and a half (to date). But so far, all have left at some point.

Lone Eagle was our first helper, and definitely the most knowledgeable. He had done all his farming with horses, and was highly entertaining (especially after consuming 40 ounces of alcohol). He pulled into Gateway on his first day, parked just past the front entrance in a grove of aspen, and lived in a made-over Safeway truck for just about a year. He was very talented at woodworking, and raised our posts and beams and built rail fences in addition to helping me with the horses. Then he'd retire each evening to his Taj Mahal to down a bottle of whatever was handy. Not surprisingly, there were good days and bad days.

Lone Eagle was immaculate in his housekeeping, and he liked to bake bread. He used very little water—in fact, just forty-five gal-

We are born naked, vulnerable, innocent, and completely safe, and we spend the rest of our days protecting ourselves—from what? Fear of the unknown? We knew nothing before we got here, and we made it to birth okay. I must challenge any fear or doubt; run naked into truth—no small mission. So what is the remaining hurdle? That last bit of ego; that last bit of doubt in a concept I fully know to be true; that lapse into forgetfulness—the human condition. "Looking for love" the first book of my life, and "Naked into Truth" the second.

To translate the gift of finding love in all life into the workable solution of running naked into truth. Now that I have found God (Love) everywhere, the test is to live by my beliefs, to translate those into form. To create a work of art with every fiber of my being.

"Thou shall know them by the fruit they bear . . . bear witness to me."

lons a week, which he got in a big drum—but somehow he was always clean and well groomed, as were the horses. There was the odd binge, when we had to check to see if he was still alive, but generally he had a heart of gold, even though it was sometimes buried beneath his gruff exterior.

"Been in jail twice," he would say, and we would, with great trepidation, ask why, only to be treated to a two-hour story that always exonerated him at the very least. I did encourage him to write a book, to share his many stories. For instance, there was the time when he lived in his pickup truck for a year, surviving on sardines and Mr. Noodles. His sojourn in Pemberton, British Columbia, was his longest, where he built a farm with his Percherons and drove into town in his wagon for supplies and a visit to the local saloon. He was a faller, a timber framer, an inventor, and an expert with leather; he made everything from dresses to saddles. I was enthralled and perplexed. He kept our property together for our fledgling year, helped us through the winter (he had lived up north for a year or two), and shaped the path the ranch would take.

After listening to all of Lone Eagle's stories, I couldn't understand why such a talented person had experienced such bad luck. He had built three homesteads alone, and all had burned down for different reasons—some suspicious, some not. (The latter gave me cause to reflect toward the end of our relationship, when Lone Eagle was growing increasingly grumpy.) Anyway, he convinced me that Gateway's fortune lay in offering wagon-ride excursions and barbecues in the hills beyond. I was convinced, so I bought Percherons and harnesses, and paid him to build a wagon—all of which cost me dearly.

The wagon was beautiful, but I never learned to drive it. I preferred direct contact with the horses. Nothing like a good Percheron between your legs. Millie and Pearl were their names, and Millie, shortly after arriving, gave birth to Freddie, a Welsh pony/Percheron cross. Figure this out: The Welsh pony was the dad. (I've seen Millie get down on her knees, so I know how it happened.) In fact, Millie got down on her knees quite often when I first started riding her. She was slightly smaller than Pearl, which was why she was my favorite. They both had the most wonderful personalities, and were, in fact, thrilled to leave the wagon behind, and gallop in the hills. Millie had one trick she used to pull when she grew tired of being ridden. She could drop down from a trot, ask the rider to get off by shifting her weight to one side, and then

Nothing like a good Percheron between your legs

rise and resume her gait in about ten seconds flat. I, of course, found this entertaining and endearing, since I already loved her, but I taught her to stop doing it for safety's sake. I just remained seated when she asked for the dismount, and suggested she get back up. We only had to do it twice.

Millie and I shared some of the most fun I have ever had on horseback. She was kind, sensible, and although the ground shook when she galloped, I was wedged safely on her broad back, confident I'd never come off. There was no danger of her doing something stupid, so I honed my bareback and halter riding as she carried me through the hills.

We did give four or five wagon rides, but they did not make us wealthy. Percherons, in fact, eat just about what they bring in, and the girls were putting on weight, being privy to the free-feed program I had put in place for the Warmbloods.

Freddy was my darling. I could drape myself across his pudgy mattress of

Look out!

a back, and he would take me anywhere. However, he presented something of a health and safety risk with his Percheron body and Welsh legs. The problem, from Kevin's perspective, was the shortness of Freddy's legs, which allowed him to go pretty much anywhere. He regularly limboed under the paddock gate, and touched the untouchables in the horse-free zone.

I remember one day when a set of wealthy friends came to visit in their shiny new Range Rover. They took the required tour of the "petting" zoo, stayed for lunch, and as they were about to depart in their pride and joy, Kevin happened to notice tracks across the hood that looked to be about the size of Freddy's teeth. Kevin, of course, didn't bring this to our friends' attention, and we always wondered whether the insurance company had solved the mystery. (This reminds me of another time when our children and their friends, who used to jump from the deck to the trampoline below, had decided the van roof nearby looked inviting. The insurance company was thinking alien attack, and we ourselves didn't find out the real cause until our son Peter confessed years later.)

Freddy and the "Perchies" (as they were affectionately known) stayed for a little over two years. Lone Eagle then talked me into another investment folly: the Gatehouse. This structure was quickly designed by Kevin, as was his way with our home improvement projects, being too busy on Millionaires Row to give more than a weekend to any personal projects. Kevin is very talented, however, and can do a pretty good job in that amount of time. It was originally going to be Lone Eagle's workshop, leather shop, and gift shop/meeting place for the wagon rides. This plan lasted for about a week, until Lone Eagle drove his Safeway truck into the sunset, afraid of the commitment. He had gotten very cranky, and had decided it was time to move on. Nonetheless, he had built the yardstick by which we would measure his successors. Kevin had to book another weekend to make drastic changes to the Gatehouse plans (which is probably why he didn't invest more than two days in the first place

So Lone Eagle left, and we were in for a succession of wagon-driver wannabes. First on the list was Brad.

Brad had bravado. He showed up, a bundle of nerves, chain-smoking (which we told him he was not allowed to do in the dry country), and drinking coffee to settle his nerves when not allowed to smoke. Brad knew it all, and had done it all. Talk about a recipe for disaster with horses! We could see our insurance doubling as we watched him pigheadedly drive the wagon through the fence instead of the gate, leaving the back half of the wagon to replace the break.

"You're fired!" I said, feeling fortunate to be alive.

The day before, he had yelled, "LOOK OUT!" at the top of his lungs (because he was a nervous wreck and a horse was walking out of the barn). I stood at the barn door, watching six previously calm horses stampede outside to see what was the matter. Lucky they love me. This was a huge lesson as to how quickly horses can mirror the energy that surrounds them. My herd is rarely ever concerned with goings-on around the barn; things get dropped on the floor above, workmen arrive and start projects. If the horses are at all nervous, I invite them over to meet the workers and watch for a while. Usually, a few minutes later, when they see I'm not bothered, they are resting their heads on workers' shoulders or picking up tools to help. Truly bombproof horses like mine will eat quietly with compressors and nail guns at work on the barn wall. Brad, however, got the horses so stirred up that the Perchies pulled the wagon in a wavy line, and the passengers wanted to take out life insurance before boarding.

My herd is rarely ever concerned with goings-on around the barn; things get dropped on the floor above, workmen arrive and start projects. If the horses are at all nervous, I invite them over to meet the workers and watch for a while. Usually, a few minutes later, when they see I'm not bothered, they are resting their heads on workers' shoulders or picking up tools to help.

Next was Sue. Remember the Johnny Cash song, "A Boy named Sue"? Well, our Sue wore some unusual and eye-catching outfits that spoke of a softer, feminine side, particularly the cropped tops that allowed her softness to spill over the tight span-dex bottoms, tucked into cowboy boots. Sue was still one of the boys, however, and always had been. She had been known to beat up her brothers, and in the end, when she threatened to beat me up, I ran and hid behind Freddy. She left in disgust at my defenselessness. I was always task-by-gender-orient-ed. Sue left in her wake a series of bear sightings, as the garbage she strewed along the way would have rivaled the city dump.

Enough barn help for now—back to the Perchies. I loved them dearly, almost to the detriment of my young Warmbloods. Being able to stay on your seat rather than your toes while riding the Perchies was a plus. Alas, they were also the epitome of "easy keepers." The three Perchies gorging on one side of the hay feeder left no room for the Warmbloods. I was forced to make a decision when I realized the Perchies' lives were at stake. Founder (lameness brought on by overeating), is not a pretty sight, and they were well on their way.

Fortunately, the perfect home materialized: a young couple who farmed with horses on their beautiful spread in Lillooet wanted the Perchies. When they came to get Millie and Pearl, I was heartsick for Freddy. He had cut his teeth nursing on both his mom and his aunt, and at the age of two was con-tinuing to do so. The couple brought their daughters, ages two and five. After running this rather large gift past her parents, I asked Megan, the older girl, if she wanted to ride Freddy, and she hopped up, legs in a perfect split, grabbed the halter rope, and off they rode. Millie and Pearl heaved a huge sigh of relief when Freddy pushed between their legs into the trailer and grabbed first one teat and then the other. I managed, between racking sobs, to tell myself that they would live happily ever after, and I believe that they will.

SURRENDER
[Channeled journal entry]

It's not what you expected, is it?
When you surrender to the current,
life takes a direction of its own.
Our life
becomes a creation, a joy, and a
free flow.
Each day a new beginning; a new
growing and becoming. You are
traveling
quickly now—don't look back, and
most of all, don't fear the appear-
ance.
You have asked me to be with you,
and
I am there. You will no longer see
the illusions if you truly know
that—
it's all one, you see. Joy and sorrow
depend only on your vantage point.
This is your creation—
don't be afraid
to be who you are.
When the time is
right, it will all come together,
and you
will see the whole perspective, and
you will see how much I love you;
for now, be content.

Chapter 6

With Heartfelt Thanks
THE GIFT IN ALL THINGS

WE HAD BEEN ON OUR RANCH FOR THREE YEARS by this time. Gateway had been affectionately nicknamed "Gatewhirl" by Kevin, with his twisted sense of humor. His clients, who by now had built significant spreads across Stump Lake, had also become friends. It was ideal to have periods of solitude and meditation, and then a rush of visitors on the weekends or holidays.

Then there was the guest ranch itself, just ten minutes away, so we never felt too alone. There was never a dull moment, with lots of parties and free-form entertainment. Derek, the more gregarious partner in the ranch, was the front man of the operation. Dabbling in cattle and cowboys, he was generous to a fault. King of the real estate marketing and hospitality business, he threw large bashes complete with popular bands for thousands of guests. Later, when the sawdust had settled, he realized that he had dispensed far more liquor and food than made sense for the lucrative running of a guest ranch, so he moved on to other projects. Lisa and Matt, a young and very competent couple, took over the management of the guest ranch, which still runs today.

Several of our new friends had also acquired horses, so my

WITH HEARTFELT THANKS

For me, having horses is not just about riding and training and competition, but about the special relationship we share with them, and the pure joy of smelling, touching, and basking in their presence.

I cherish the quiet times: When I am privileged to watch a birth, and my mare welcomes me, and trusts me to cradle her baby, or when the rest of the herd crowds around the birthing stall, stretching their necks, each longing for a sniff or a lick of the new baby. Or the first time I sit on one of my young horses—just slide on from a nearby fence—and he turns and looks at me puzzled, and nuzzles my foot. When these powerful, majestic creatures carry me bareback and haltered safely where I ask, or allow me to accompany them on an adventure of their choice, or when I walk out in the fields to find them and they all come over to greet me, I am honored, and I am forever amazed that such magnificent beings agreeably submit to my will.

barn help had the additional responsibility of looking after those horses on their land when their owners were away (which was most of the time). Rather like an episode of *Lifestyles of the Rich and Famous*, a visit to Millionaires Row provided a sharp contrast to our simple lifestyle. In architecturally stunning houses, each one bigger than the last, they had the best of the best of everything, but since these were generally third or fourth homes, visits were sometimes few and far between.

Some, however, like Shirley and her husband Gordon, became close friends. Jane, a lifelong friend, bought a ranch as well, and April and Clive, our good friends for years, had also visited and wanted to spend more time here. This lifestyle was infectious. Shirley bought L.E.'s second baby, Raphael, and April bought Mira's first baby, Luxury Edition (Luxy). This led to April and Clive taking out a long-term lease at the Gatehouse, where they would frequently stay. Shirley preferred to transport Raffi and her other horse via trailer, back and forth from their ranch to their property near Vancouver. We girls talked horses constantly, driving our not-so-horsey husbands to distraction. We would leave the boys to their own discourse and gather at the other end of the room, talking about the passion that had taken over our lives.

The step we all took together was to become involved in Parelli Natural Horsemanship, which is a system that teaches you and your horse to work together in partnership through various levels of development. We found a talented teacher and made a commitment to attend one or two clinics each year. This evolved into a private clinic that was held at Gateway for just the four of us (and occasionally, other friends), an event we still look forward to every year. For five days we immerse ourselves in a good eight hours of learning and fun each day, followed by a barbecue and a lot of laughs. Jonathan, our teacher, makes jokes about my somewhat softened and embellished version of the "Seven Games" (the basis of Parelli's teachings about understanding the language of horses).

I started my Parelli partnership program with Prima. Although she was imprinted, well loved, and kindly trained by normal methods, she was inherently suspicious, and at the same time somewhat haughty from her apparent past life as a princess. (Prima's name was even more apt if you added a "Donna" on the end.) However, a strange thing started to happen once we began the program. The more I gently insisted on our relationship evolving to a regular

Prima visiting Mom

"In one instant you can change the world. If man were to change his mind; one mind at a time, a chain reaction (like nuclear fission) would occur. Human minds like ours, are all joined. It is a belief in isolation that creates the limits. Simply let them go and a far greater world is yours, ours, and in the communion of spirit as it has always been."

—Premiere Edition (Prima)
Speaking for the Herd

schooling session for the both of us, the more cooperative she grew. I made it fun for her, and rewarding, but sometimes by being firm and insisting she try the exercise, I encouraged a higher level of her respect, and with it, her affection. She loved it when I appeared to know what we were supposed to do, and my translation to her involved her continued growth and learning. She was becoming

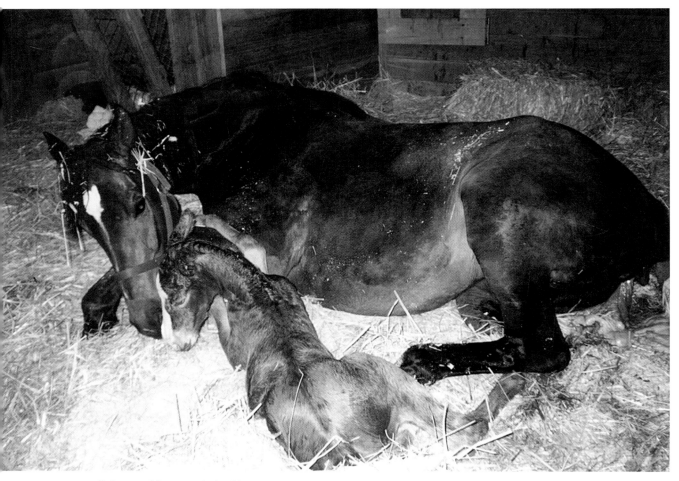

Prima and her new baby, Epona

"There are two ends to the spectrum. Fear is one end and it is false.

Love is at the other end and it is all that is true."

—Premiere Edition (Prima)
Speaking for the Herd

more and more confident, both in her relationship to the herd, and to me.

I started using an exercise called Liberty more and more. Instead of the 22-foot rope and carrot stick to get her to circle, I could use a pretend rope and simply a hand gesture where the stick had been. I extended this to play outside the round pen, and before long I could lead her without a halter, and ask her to move various parts of her body with just a look. I experimented with holding images of the required action in my mind, and she would do it faster. The slightest tip of my head would send her backwards. She began to mimic me, and when I walked forward or back, so would she. We ventured further from the herd, and she would trot behind me, over jumps and bridges, and she would leap confidently onto giant tires. This growing trust was always cemented by lots of treats, although she performed these tasks without treats as well, and Prima would politely groom me to release the treat.

Activities that I once thought impossible were completed by Prima with ease and confidence, such as when she allowed me to bridle or halter her from my knees (or while mounted), and when we rode figure eights and backed with just a string around her neck. This progressed to trail rides, bareback with a halter; the more rope I gave her, the less she needed. Very important was the word "whoa," and she had to back to where the word was said if she took a few steps after the command. My horse and I were having fun together; we were partners.

My herd was becoming interested in the proceedings, and one by one, they began to ask to be included. Prima's firstborn, Epona, was named after the horse goddess, and she is my darling. When she was born at three in the morning, I was slightly delirious, and initially proclaimed her a boy. I also thought her unattractive, being a somewhat golden-gray color in the light, and of course, slightly squished from the birth. Her spirit was unmistakable, however. While still inside her mother, she had tried to climb out. During the birth, while Prima paced with the baby in her birth canal, feet hanging out, Epona was trying to clamber out of her mother. At last, I helped her out, and Epona has since looked upon me as her mother. I was the first person she saw, and I introduced her to her horse mom, who was just managing to lift her head after the ordeal.

It wasn't until the next morning that I wistfully lifted the baby's tail to double-check the gender, and was delighted to find that she was, in fact, a girl. That meant I could keep this baby, who had suddenly grown more beautiful to me. As a breeder, I knew I had to sell my colts, but Epona now had the chance to win me over completely, and that she did. Maybe it was the contrast of her coloring, after six or so dark bays (which had been my favorite color). Suddenly, I had a blonde! As she grew, her mane and tail lightened, and by six

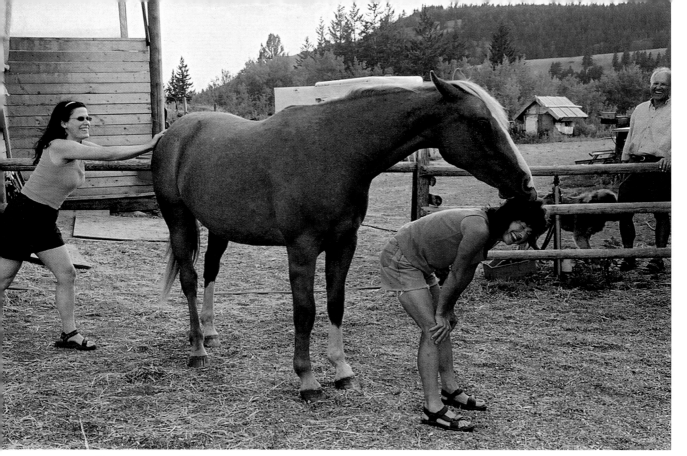

You groom me, I'll groom you

months, I had a palomino. Trigger, my first love, had resurfaced.

As a filly, Epona was in every way a goddess. She ruled over the colts, Leo and Raffi (the latter L.E.s' baby). My neighbor Shirley bought Raffi as a year-ling, and Leo was sold to Nikki, a wonderful rider with an ideal home.

I am thinking that Epona will probably be my last horse (since I'll be eighty in twenty-six years, and I can't hope to ride much beyond that age). She is also flawless, possessing all of her mother's wonderful qualities and none of her baggage. Epona was the first to become engaged in my natural horseman-ship program. She watched her mother enjoy the attention and treats, and she'd fight to squeeze through the gate when I worked with her mom. Full of bravado, without a halter or lead, she would follow me across the property, about a mile-and-a-half walk, before she was two. When we went for rides she would follow along without a rider. She was particularly fond of treats, so when I said "Stick to me," there was no antidote. She would run over and jump on a tire if we were in the vicinity. Most of all, she showed no fear; each new experience was met with openness and curiosity. If I let her out of the paddock (into the horse-free zone), she would follow me around to the house, and if I had left the door open, she certainly would have moved right in. After some time spent clumping around on the deck, she would fall asleep, her head on the glass door. If there was ever a horse that I wanted to move into my living room, it was Epona.

The first time I saddled her, she didn't even pay attention, and when I mounted, she turned around to say, "If you're up there, how do I access the treats?" She is sane, sensible, and a joy to ride. How could I improve on this perfect genotype? Perhaps with her brother, Picasso (even though he will have to be sold). Two years her junior, this colt is also a model child. At present, he is just seven months old, outgoing and friendly, and leaves the herd in a flash. He will trot or canter quite happily behind me, racing out of the gate before another horse steals the show. He follows me to the adventure playground, the horse amusement park, with bridges, jumps, sand-filled tires, and various bombproofing materials like hula skirts hanging from trees, balloons, tarps, and so on. He will move any part and back at a glance, jumping small logs and stopping on a dime.

Matisse, Picasso's best friend, is a year older. Very self-assured as well, Matisse is happy to spend his time in human company. He will follow me to the riding ring (twice as far as the adventure playground), and he's fluent in all the other games.

I am beginning to wonder if this success with the babies is due to just my breeding protocol (i.e., imprinting and daily handling), or is it my ever-increasing horse awareness and connection being reflected through the herd? Horses are a lot like geese—interwoven in their patterns; dancing together as one; knowing and sensing as one.

I have watched my mares talking to their unborn babies. It starts happening when they are about seven months pregnant. They nicker to them in their sleep, and they know exactly to whom they are talking. I can tell as well now. I start talking to the

I AM SO JOY-FULL

I am beginning to believe (actually live) that everything is perfect— no deadlines, no pressure. Just being in the moment; feeling the joy of being.
"Thou shall love the Lord, thy God, with all thy heart, and all thy mind,
And all thy strength, and thy neighbor as thyself."

I do—and I am filled with such JOY. Every small thing is so miraculous, such a gift: the sun, the warm wind, the softness in Epona's eye. The gift of friends— lovely people, small perfect little creatures—the little white ermine with the black tip on his tail that ran out of my garbage box. The hugeness and gentleness of Pearl and Millie. The generosity of friends and family. The perfection of each and every moment, and the gift in all things.
Drifting down the river in the sun—perfect analogy.
I am so very happy!
I am so very happy!

babies at about the same time. I talk to the tummy and name the boy or girl before they are born. I can see what they look like. I have so far been right. (I called Epona a girl throughout gestation; it wasn't until her birth that I misjudged and thought for a day that she was a boy!) It just occurred to me the other day how this could be possible: Animals communicate by projecting telepathic picture ideas, so of course they know what their unborn babies look like, and therefore, can show me as well.

Always thought to be a little on the fringe by many of my friends, I often consult with my animal psychic friends for backup. I even hosted an animal body-talk and communication workshop one summer. There were about fifteen or so practitioners, and they were very impressed with my horses. My horses were in turn impressed with the workshop, and it offered valuable possibilities, as well as a lot of fun. I still use body talk whenever one of my horses has a problem. Body talk establishes a healthy mind-body connection that enables a natural state of health.

Matisse, born with a contracted tendon and a subsequent clubfoot, is completely normal now at age two. Although the vets had recommended cutting ligaments and tendons, I tapped him out with body talk and miraculously, he is perfect with no surgery. The vets remark on it whenever they visit.

When she was a year old, Epona injured her foot, losing the front inside quarter on a rock. Again, I body-talked, and with the aid of a therapeutic farrier, she is fine today. I believe the brain, having the ability to create perfection in new life, is also capable of re-creating it where necessary.

> I still use body talk whenever one of my horses has a problem. Body talk establishes a healthy mind-body connection that enables a natural state of health.

Another professional who visits regularly is the chiropractor, and I am always impressed by the difference a readjustment makes. L.E. cantered like a crab before I realized that it was in her spine and not her mind. Something unseen, like roughhousing in the pasture or a difficult birth, can cause a problem in the spine, which subsequently affects the gait. I have had some of my horses come around in just one treatment, and I'm convinced that regular visits are a necessity.

I have also employed massage therapists and healing-touch practitioners to treat my horses—in fact, any modality that I would use for myself, I will try

Picasso — first premium at his inspection

on my horses. Generally, though, their lifestyle is reflected in their good health. Because they graze freely on a large acreage, they have not needed worming since we moved here. (I do worm them for bots—which don't always show up in fecal samples, so I do them to be safe—in the fall only.)

I think our biggest trauma to date was when Diva lost her twins. As a breeder, I have always been advised to use ultrasound to check for twins. When Diva was checked, the vet said that one twin was considerably smaller, and would most likely be absorbed. Consequently, she was too far along when we found out that this hadn't happened, and she lost her babies at nine months. One was born dead; the other gravely ill.

Never have I seen such devastation in a horse. In retrospect, I think I made the wrong choice: I left her with the dead twin, and took the live one (who the vet said couldn't possibly make it) into the tack room, and tried to keep him comfortable and warm. I was worried Diva would try to get him to

Matisse and Magic — first meeting

stand up when he couldn't, since the cartilage in his legs was unformed. (He died soon after.)

I have since reconsidered; he was, after all, her baby, and Diva grieved for months, nickering every time I saw her, seeming to ask me where the baby was. I found out years later (when Diva told a psychic friend) that she thought she had killed her first baby, and that I hadn't trusted her with the second one. At her next birth with Magic, she broke out of the birthing stall and retreated to the safety of the pasture, where she thought with more room, she couldn't hurt her baby. I hope she knows now that the death of her twins wasn't her fault.

I wonder at people who think animals are not capable of the level of emotion that humans are. Along with the joys, breeding has its share of sorrow, and last year L.E. also lost a baby. She had a difficult birth, and I had to pull the baby into the world. Three days later, the foal died of an enlarged heart,

Diva and Cleo

"Boundaries are thoughts and create limits in a limitless universe.

When boundaries dissolve, opportunities expand."

—Premiere Edition (Prima)
Speaking for the Herd

and L.E. stood guard over her, unable to believe she wouldn't get up again. L.E. is eight months pregnant now, and I am so hoping for a girl; L.E. loves her babies forever. Prima, her firstborn, is still her best friend. They groom each other, eat together, and share family time with children and grandchildren. That is so important in the herd, to be able to groom and play, or just stand together guarding the sleeping babies.

I see stabled horses in their individual paddocks, electric fence between, never enjoying even a friendship, let alone these strong family ties. That is why I find it so difficult to sell my babies. I have so far found wonderful homes for some of my horses. Leo has a wonderful partner. Nikki is devoted to her horses, a strong rider, and believes they should all have the same kind of life as I do. Friends, freedom, and lots of love are as important to horses as they are to us. Luxy, now five, has been owned by my friend, April, for three years. She believes Luxy's relationship with her herd is as important as their relationship with each other, so April spends a lot of time with her here, instead of moving her to the city for the sake of convenience.

WHAT A FEELING

First when there's nothing
but a slow glowing dream
that your fear seems to hide
deep inside your mind.

All alone I have cried
silent tears full of pride
in a world made of steel,
made of stone.

Well, I hear the music,
close my eyes, feel the rhythm,
wrap around, take a hold
of my heart.

What a feeling.
Bein's believin'.
I can have it all, now I'm dancing for my life.
Take your passion
and make it happen.
Pictures come alive, you can dance right through your life.

Chapter 7

Learning to Leap
LIVING BY THE PRINCIPLES

T HE YEARS, MARKED CLEANLY BY THE SEASONS, began to involve activities that were dependent on the calendar. For Christmas each year we would make a Gateway calendar, with either seasonal photographs of the property taken by Kevin, or photographs of the horses that I'd taken. The first notations on my calendar were always the birth dates of my babies, generally in April, May, and June, and then the breeding cycles of my mares who were being bred for the following year. Eleven months' gestation is such a long wait. Since moving to the ranch, our horse numbers have continued to change.

We found wonderful homes for our two geldings whom we had brought with us. Mira had Luxy the first spring. The Perchies and Freddy came and went. Prima had Epona, L.E. had Raffi, and Mira had Leo. The following spring, Diva had her second foal, Magic, and Mira gave birth to Matisse. I sold some of the foals, but of all of those babies, two are still with me. My answer to Kevin's rising alarm was, of course, that these were valuable horses and this was a business that would eventually pay off. His retort was always, of course, "When?"

Breeding is not always successful. Last year, L.E. lost her baby, and Mira aborted, so there was only Picasso born last spring. This

LEARNING TO LEAP

Had four adventure dreams all in one night . . .

The first: I was riding L.E. bareback with no reins. I kept sliding off backwards, but I was floating on the air behind her and kept pulling myself back on . . .

The second: Kevin is pushing me off a high wharf. I'm on the way down, and I don't really want to hit the water, but I'm comfortable and resigned (I'm on the way down, after all). We do this several times, and then I notice a big buoy in the water below me. I adjust my fall to avoid it.

The third: We are playing a full-size adventure game. Kevin and I and two others are at the opening door (much like an elevator). Everyone is afraid to go in. I step in, unafraid, and Kevin follows me. There is a door to the next compartment and I walk in. As it starts to close behind us, Kevin pulls me out. I think everyone is silly to be afraid. I feel totally safe and I'm going to play the game myself.

The fourth: We are playing hide-and-seek. The rules are, we move with our feet a couple of inches off the ground so we don't leave any tracks! It's cold out and I am in a T-shirt and bare feet, thinking this is perfectly natural for me.

year I've bred five mares. Our difficult past year coincided with the arrival of our latest barn help, or as she prefers to be called, "horse concierge," Suzanna. Prior to Suzanna's arrival, we had a brief stint with Rigit, who was as weird as her name, and lasted the shortest time of all, just three weeks.

Then there deserves to be a brief mention of Magi. She thought herself somewhat of a magician with horses, and would tell me what the horses had told her. This never coincided with what I had intuited, and I felt I knew them better. Magi would tell me the horses needed such-and-such, but when she acquired and presented this much-desired and hard-to-pronounce "ingredient" (usually some herb or supplement), the horses would walk away, leaving it to collect dust. Magi began to get cranky, and the horses tested her sorely. There was a lot of wheelbarrow tipping, some intimidation by Prima, and it all culminated in Magi "communicating" by waving a hay rake at the horses. I did suggest to her that since she and the horses understood each other so well, perhaps she might try talking it over. But by then they had left the bargaining table, and Magi's crankiness had escalated to absolute paranoia. She started carrying a gun over her shoulder when she walked to the barn each day. There could be bears or coyotes, she claimed, but I experienced increasing anxiety that she would shoot my dog by accident, or possibly a horse who had tipped her wheelbarrow once too often. Exit Magi!

My barn help had now become the talk of the town. The feed store I dealt with was ready to demand ID, there had been so many different faces picking up grain. It was the first question asked by visiting friends or family, and generally a source of amusement for the local gossips.

I became wary. We advertised and interviewed, but it was not going well. Then Suzanna and Steve arrived. Nineteen and twenty-four years old, respectively: very young, very nice, and happily, they appeared to be quite normal. I hired them because Suzanna insisted, and as my horses will tell you, I'm a pushover. (In their case, this is sometimes literal!) I'm lucky Suzanna did insist, because ten months later, Steve is gone, but she is still here, responsible, neat, conscientious, a strong rider, and a great all-around horse person. She is also learning Parelli with the rest of us, and is as open to exploring anything to do with horses as I am.

Suzanna believes in tough love, and has no problem going to Phase 4 (which in Parelli is asking with as much force as necessary to get the expected

First ride—Gabriel, Francesca, and Epona

"Life is not a struggle — at least not to the rest of us. You struggle; you believe that there is something you must accomplish. There is nothing to accomplish except the desired results of your desires."

—Premiere Edition (Prima)
Speaking for the Herd

result) or any other form of kind but firm discipline (especially when Prima nips her in the boob!) This is good, because I can remain the benevolent one, and send the naughty horse to the round pen with Suzanna. We joke about this, but there is a degree of truth in it. I believe we are learning from each other about the so-called middle way.

The horses' accommodations (always first priority) have been continually improved upon and refined. However, our quarters (referring to the size of

ONE WITH THE HERD   **125**

"Secret Garden"— painting by the author

"Beauty and Light" — painting by the author

our imprint on the overall structure, 1,100 square feet) are still in limbo. Originally, this house was designed in a big hurry when we had three months before winter to build roads, fences, wells, and other structures on our pristine land. We had a general idea that we would live there for a year or two, while building our dream home at the top of the surrounding hill. Although the view was breathtaking, over time I realized that the most beautiful sight to me was that of my horses' faces, looking up at me each morning. Another reason for our inertia was the fact that we had spent every penny on the horses' accommodations. Kevin and I still toss around plans to someday finish our floors and replace the construction stairs, but as yet, the wood is still stored in the top of the barn, and lately we have been discussing an addition to our present home (which I hope will include a guest suite for Epona), instead of building up on the hill.

This would be an upgrade, with geothermal heat to augment our woodstove, and enough power from the wind and sun to allow for a large, comfortable kitchen, and a few more amenities, like drying racks for laundry (I now hang it over the stair railing). When we first talked solar, we were going to build our own refrigerated space, and research solar dishwashers and such; but since this was to be just a temporary space, we opted for the largest propane fridge available (which is the size fridges were fifty years ago), and a propane stove on the same scale.

Propane is the bane of my existence. It makes me very nervous. You have only to read the caution stickers on any of the appliances to acquire this fear. Add to this a finicky propane generator and a propane heater in the tack room, and I have cause for a lot of gray hairs when my husband is away. It seems that every time Kevin has been away for a couple of days in the winter, I have had an emergency situation (at least, that's how it registers to me in my panicky state). I don't read instructions well, I cannot light pilot lights, and I'm dyslexic when it comes to mechanical or electrical gadgetry.

We have a modern version of the Rubik's Cube, called a "magic box," and it holds a jigsaw puzzle of pieces that systematically tests your sanity. The magic box is supposed to be the mastermind of the solar system, generator, and water tanks, so that all components will interact nicely and solve all of our problems. Instead, this has become our biggest problem. The magic box does not always do what it's supposed to, and Kevin doesn't always know why.

Neither do most of the electricians we have opened accounts with, to try and decipher its mysteries.

When Kevin is away and the magic box acts up, things fall apart rapidly. Horse water freezes, generators won't start, it gets cold and dark, and I panic. I then have to follow instructions over the phone, like put a hot plate under the generator and warm it up. This involves fire and propane—two things that I'm sure shouldn't mix. I remember calling a gas company once when I couldn't light the pilot light on the stove, certain we had a broken gas line. I had the man worried enough to tell me to grab the animals and stand out in the foot-deep snow at minus-20 degrees. The hour-long trip to our house revealed it to be nothing more than my not being able to light the pilot. Better safe than sorry, and the nice man took me around and showed me how to turn off the gas line at the important junctions for future reference.

I'm actually adept with wood fires and natural hardships; it's the gadgetry I don't trust. If you have ever examined the back of a propane fridge, it's definitely cause for worry. It looks like a high school science project, with tinfoil ducts and tubing that runs through your cupboards to the outside, where it drips rust down your roof (hokey, to say the least). This year Kevin made a few changes, and I was allowed an electric fridge—not a subzero like all the homes next door, but an energy-efficient, enormous refrigerator by comparison to what we'd had. It's actually too big for our kitchen, which isn't saying much. I can't believe that I now consider a normal refrigerator a blessing. Previously during the winter, our front hall housed the overload from our last fridge, but in summer, the folks from Millionaires Row would complain at our lack of ice for their martinis or vodka and cranberry.

> We're living this simple life all because I love horses, and the quality of life I share with them in this natural setting. Let me rephrase this: I worship the gifts of "HORSE," and when I put it all in perspective, I would make the choice again. There is really no other way for me to find my truth.

I do take such pleasure in simple things. Things we take for granted, like dishwashers, built-in vacuums, bread makers, and popcorn machines, have a new status called "in my fondest dreams." I could never have enough solar power for a self-cleaning oven. We're living this simple life all because I love horses, and the quality of life I share with them in this natural setting. Let me rephrase this: I worship the gifts of "HORSE," and when I put it all in perspective, I would make the choice again. There is really no other way for me to find my truth.

If I won the lottery, we could afford 320 acres in the middle of town, but then I couldn't wake to the melodic trill of blackbirds, or be surrounded by miles of the most beautiful hills, lakes, and forests that you could ever imagine. And there is the quality of the air and the quiet.

When I follow the horses and sit on a hill watching them graze against a backdrop of endless sky, I am filled with such peace and joy. I wouldn't trade this for anything. The words of the Twenty-third Psalm come to life here: my cup truly runneth over.

Chapter 8

Feeling is Believing
MANIFESTATION

I have always been very right-brained, and consequently, technologically challenged, as I have no interest in removing the cobwebs from the left. How challenged I am I really can't say, being sufficiently challenged to not really absorb the parameters. Kevin has noted that although messages travel back and forth from right to left brain millions of times a day in ordinary people, my exchanges are reduced to maybe just two or three.

Being right-brained, I am told, runs hand in hand with creativity, and I suppose this is what led me to my path as an artist. Having moved to a constant source of inspiration, on acres of unbelievable beauty and variety, I began to immerse myself in my surroundings. My art spoke more and more of horses in their natural setting, horses at rest and at play, captured in their many moods. Passion, Freedom, Reflection, Beauty and Light, and Glory were some of the titles of my paintings. I was expressing my own immersion in the land, as well as the spirit of the horse.

To my husband's and children's chagrin. They were not so enamoured with the reclusive lifestyle that I had chosen and they were increasingly jealous of my affection for the horses. I was more and more content to live in the comfort of my herd, and my land. The simplicity of the lifestyle was increasingly seductive, and I found myself more and more removed from material trappings,

FEELING IS BELIEVING
(Channeled journal entry)

Elizabeth—always looking for me, never trusting that you have me already. I am always with you. It is good that you find me everywhere; in my creatures, my creations.

You, my dear, are the Create-or—which means you have a choice in what you want to see.
You are always stretching your limits by what you choose to experience; lately, you have stretched immensely. The same themes surface again and again in your life: "Looking for Love," and "Naked into Truth." You are feeling open, vulnerable. You are trusting, and with trust comes a letting go of your guard, your shield that protects you from the world. You are safe; welcome the tears, which wash away your impurities. To be pure you must be open. When you are open, you are bathed in spiritual energy. When there is no definition between us, then there is only one.

Elizabeth, you have asked, and I am taking the steps toward you. Welcome me with open arms. Speak the truth; the truth that sings loud and clearly in your heart.

What a feeling; being's believing.

either for comfort or retreat. Well-broken-in jeans, a shirt, and a good pair of boots became my staples, and communing with my land and my creatures, my solace. There was a secret here: I'd discovered that my lifelong search for my Holy Grail was actually an attainable obsession. I was beginning to understand the miraculous connection between thought and manifestation. I had only to recognize my heart's desire for it to materialize in every detail.

Now my intent was directed toward communication. I was feeling more and more that we each wear our own magic glasses, and reality is unique to our individual life path. Almost as quickly as I focused on a particular desire, it would materialize before my eyes.

One remarkable example appeared on a rafting trip down the Rio Grande River. This was a "once-a-year trip" that Kevin had coerced me to take. It was March, during the spring thaw, and we had left the brown soggy plains of Gateway for the sunny skies of the Texas/Mexico border. I was reading a Sylvia Browne book at the time about life paths, and white and dark entities, and complaining daily about the absence of horses. Even a burro would have been greatly appreciated.

I was stretched across the broad wall of the raft, tanning and reading, oblivious to most of the scenery, when suddenly, for no reason, I sat up and asked our trip leader, Ian, "Where are we?" It was the first expression of interest I had shown in the trip.

Ian answered, "Cavallo Blanco Canyon." White Horse Canyon. And although I thought this name must surely refer to just a rock form of a white horse (after all, how could a horse live long enough to be featured in the tour guide?), I nevertheless was keenly alert, camera in hand.

Suddenly, there it was. The canyon walls were steep right up to the river, but ahead was a spit of land, with green grass turned golden in a shaft of sunlight, where a white horse was standing. I was amazed. As we drifted closer the horse began to nod. All else became invisible to me, except for the nodding white horse on its tiny spit of meadow. Then as we passed a darkly shadowed thicket, there stood a black horse, hidden but for a small white star on his forehead. I grabbed my camera and snapped a few pictures.

Incredulous now, I babbled incoherently to all who would listen about the serendipity of finding both a white and a dark horse in White Horse Canyon, while reading a book about white and dark entities. My rafting companions were unimpressed, to say the least, and I was left to enjoy this personal epiphany on my own. The closer we drew, the deeper the white horse bowed. I had never seen a horse do this before; it was almost mechanical in its movement, like a Disney automated horse. I'm sure that Kevin was the only one who appreciated the significance this event held for me. Horses are mirrors for our emotions and beliefs. This was a clear reflection of the culmination of both my spiritual beliefs and their reflection in my art, and my commitment to truly communicate with horses.

Following this trip, I came to see that as a horse worshipper, I was likewise being worshipped in return. My understanding of human beings' interconnection with all life became crystallized. I began to remove myself from all the distractions that would interrupt this active meditation. Living in a solar home, isolated for the most part from all that we didn't welcome, I divorced myself from the outside world. My only diversions were books and videos that related to horses and heaven—or at least the spiritual path that leads to heaven. This sense of quiet and the lack of clutter in my thoughts left me open to experiencing a more animal-like existence.

My worshipping in the religion of Horse led to many revelations that seemed, more and more, to come from the horses' perspective. Why did we feel the need to dominate and use animals for our purposes, instead of sharing in their wisdom? Could their purpose be independent of our desires, and could they have something unique and special to share with us? Was there wisdom in the simplicity of their existence, and could we have unfairly discredited them simply because they don't speak our language? Actually, it seems that it's we who are uneducated in their ways, not the other way around.

Horses' knowledge seems to exist as a cellular memory inherent in their birthright. They have not forgotten their relationship to the earth as we humans have.

Horses' knowledge seems to exist as a cellular memory inherent in their birthright. They have not forgotten their relationship to the earth as we humans have. They are wise in their reliance on instinct and emotion, for their lives as prey animals are dependent upon that. We, the predators, have relied on our intellect to trap and make use of our prey, but in so doing have deciphered their gifts through our own perspective—or at least chosen to ignore them for our own benefit. Imagine being as free as the wind, which horses are

"Humans believe in opposites; we believe in sames."

—Premiere Edition (Prima)
Speaking for the Herd

in their wild state, living in the moment; the most elusive quest for all spiritual seekers was theirs. I began to realize that to truly communicate, I had to be truly in the moment with them, whether on their backs or on the ground. It was a dance that I could learn only by following.

I remembered a dream I'd had shortly after moving to Gateway. I call it "Mr. Tambourine Man," after Bob Dylan's song: "Take me for a trip upon your magic swirling ship / all my senses have been stripped . . . I promise to go anywhere I'm ready for today / I'm in my own parade . . . Cast your dancing spell my way."

This is what animals have to teach us: the rightness of listening to our intuition, living in the moment, and experiencing true freedom.

We have taken a spiritually evolved creature whose life was choreographed to dance like the wind, and crushed their spirits by our fear, our need to control and capture. Thinking we can own their joy along with their bodies, we try to take it from them, and we crush it in the process. It is no longer theirs to share. They develop all the neuroses that thrive in captivity: cribbing, weaving, kicking, and biting their captors. Solitary confinement has taken its toll.

Imagine if you were locked in a single room, prevented from having contact with friends and family, and taken out and run around a gym a few times a week as an object of someone else's pleasure. There is no joy left in you, and you are forced to give what you no longer have. Whips, spurs, constraints—the more you fight for your freedom, the greater is your torture.

We hear stories of man's inhumanity to man with shock and disbelief, and yet this behavior is commonly thought to be perfectly acceptable where animals are concerned; whips, spurs, and confinement in a stall are commonplace. The strange thing is, we have destroyed the gifts the horses would give to us gladly. If we spent the time to truly learn their wisdom, instead of trying to bend them to our will, we would reap great rewards. It is a lose-

MR. TAMBOURINE MAN

In my dream, I am dancing in front of a tall, dark stranger. I can't see him, as he is behind me. I am facing forward and he is wrapped like a cloak around me. Our bodies fit perfectly together. I am following his every move; leaping, jumping, swirling as one. It's what I imagine it must be like to be held in God's arms: love and trust, and a sense of rightness permeate my being. This is how it is meant to be. Our minds are joined. As I think, he moves, and as he thinks, I move, completely intuitive. We are one being.

We live on fruit, and it's everywhere, all over the ground. I am picking up grapes, apples, peaches, and putting them in a basket. They are huge, perfect. Then I see big pears, but they have an imperfection by the stem. My partner tells me they aren't safe to eat, but then on the ground we find a guide with a picture of a pear, and instructions on how to eat. I believe this dream was showing me what living in the moment is truly like—how to go with the flow and find that all of your needs will be met, down to the tiniest detail.

L.E. and Epona

"Our life is like a canter; we rise and fall between realities, the spiritual and the physical in balance, with complete commitment to both."

—Premiere Edition (Prima)
Speaking for the Herd

lose situation, one we can scarcely begin to comprehend until we actually take the time to see it—the time to discover the horse's point of view. I found that the more I cleared my mind of unnecessary debris, the more open I became to horse truth.

A few years before Gateway, Kevin and I attended a four-day encounter group called "Choices: Adventures of a Lifetime." Along with about a hundred fellow participants, we were given a series of visualization exercises designed to break down barriers, and help us find positive strategies for enhancing our lives. The course really consolidated beliefs that I had developed during years of personal work. I was becoming more secure in my conclusion that life is an elaborate dream orchestrated by the higher self. Our thoughts and words have the power to change our circumstances. I came to understand the script I had written for my life at Choices, in the words to my song.

In an exercise called a "stretch," each person was given a song that was in every case the perfect one for him or her. We had to learn the words and perform them to music in front of the other participants. I, in all my glory, cut a shoulder off my sweatshirt and leapt around the stage belting out the words to "What a Feeling" from Flashdance. Luckily the music was loud enough to drown out most of my contribution.

This is natural for a horse, and the gift we could share in if we would only listen to our intuition, and live in the moment as they do.

Back at Gateway, I had a lot of field work yet to complete. It had been a long winter spent mostly reading and reflecting. The ground was warming with the spring, patches of grass showing through the melting snow, and everywhere, mud. The horses could smell the first beginnings of the new grass, and daily they wandered farther from the barn, craving the tiniest taste.

The morning the blackbirds returned, a warm wind carried their songs through the meadow, and the first hot sun began to melt the snow in earnest. Just after breakfast, the horses, one by one, lifted their heads to catch the scent, and then they were off in a long line to the hill above the front pasture.

"Redwing Blackbird" — painting by the author

The young ones, always ready for a run, were in the lead, until they reached the point of the hill overlooking the valley below, where the path turned sharply downhill. It was a sea of mud, twenty feet across and six inches deep. They came to an abrupt halt, sinking and slipping, then leaping to safe ground. I watched as they each assessed the situation, and then picking my route, I coaxed Epona, Picasso, and then Prima to follow. I was so proud of how careful they were, zigzagging cautiously from one grassy patch to the next, one step at a time. It is such an important quality for a horse to possess: taking the time to make an educated decision, and then being brave enough to follow through. The other young and athletic ones picked their way down to join us, and I watched as the adventurers took turns rolling in the snow, and chasing each other in circles, obviously pleased with themselves.

High on the hill stood the very pregnant ones, more cautious than their agile companions. L.E. was still surveying the situation. I watched her displaying the quality most important in a leader—making the right decision for the safety of the herd. The older and wiser ones were not moving until L.E. made the choice. They watched us reckless ones, and deliberated, until L.E. was sure of the best route, and with all of the big mamas in tow, she picked her way through a grassy section in the trees. All the young ones rejoiced in her arrival, and ran to join the procession as she carried straight on through to a distant meadow she thought was best.

What a lesson in leadership I had received. Take your time, make a wise choice, and proceed with conviction. L.E. sailed through life like the Queen Mary, a clear aura of power and presence visible in her every move. She was wise and thoughtful, rarely ever extending herself beyond Phase 1, which was simply placing her focus on an inattentive herd member. One look from L.E. was usually enough to warrant a quick leap out of her path and a sincere apology, in the form of a reflective lick and chew, or possibly a yawn of embarrassment from a safe distance away. L.E. was, however, completely indulgent of her children. She would move over to allow them treats, and stop in her tracks if they rudely demanded attention. This even extended to Prima's two children, who were, of course, her grandchildren.

They would pick an area like the birthing stall, which was large enough for family gatherings, and all four would eat and sleep together. I could see she missed her baby of the year before, as it would have been the same age as Picasso. On the anniversary of the death of her baby, L.E. had called for hours, running around to all the places where her baby had lain, smelling and nickering. It was painful to watch. We are all anxiously awaiting L.E.'s baby this spring.

Because L.E. is so magnificent in her position as herd leader, I love and respect her just the way she is. It would be unimaginable to me to try and dominate such a wise leader and force her into compliance. I have played join-up and the Seven Games of Parelli, and found that L.E. sees things a little differently from me. She is happy to join up, coming over and choosing to be with me, and will do so instantly, to save the unnecessary waste of energy in circling around for no reason. (She has, after all, been under my care for eight years now; I am family.) However, why would she move any part of her body away from me when she knows there is no good reason to, and she has nothing to fear?

I will not ask L.E. to do cheap parlor tricks—meaning, ask her to perform like a trained seal for human benefit. It is beneath the dignity of all animals, but even as in humans there are those who enjoy performing and there are those who do not ! (L.E. does not!) it is beneath her calling, and her dignity. She loves and respects me, and has convinced me of the frivolity of testing our relationship. We have agreed to occasional rides, and she will do anything I ask for a good reason, like standing untethered for the farrier, and politely lifting her feet, or backing or following when necessary—but performing like a trained dog is absolutely out. "This is not about egos," she will make absolutely clear, and I always respect her decision, being a privileged herd member. So much in a meaningful relationship is about give and take.

Looking For Love
LOVE VERSUS FEAR

I HAD READ ABOUT ACTIVE SAMADHI. Samadhi is a Hindu and Buddhist term that describes a non-dualistic state of consciousness, in which the consciousness of the experiencing subject becomes one with the experienced object. Baking bread, gardening, or for the most part, shoveling horse poo, was paving a clear path to horse wisdom. Just go about the simple things, relax and enjoy; they were teaching me, and in that simple truth lay real inspiration.

I was completely comfortable among my herd. I would wiggle between several large horse bodies, kissing chests or muzzles as I went. My love had grown much larger than my fear. This, of course, the horses knew, and they reflected back to me. Trainers would often remark, "That horse sure loves you." The skeptics would interpret this to mean that the horses loved the treats I always freely distributed.

I remember a heated discussion at the feed store, when I casually remarked that I always had treats in my pockets.

"I never hand-feed," one person remarked. "It teaches biting."

I answered that I believed horses, being gentle and intelligent creatures, could discriminate between a hand and a treat. In my experience they had learned to be gentle with their mouths and were extremely careful to take just the treat.

She had been looking for it as long as I could remember. As a child she had wondered, Was it something her parents could give her, hidden in a hug or a new toy, or was it beyond the confines of her home, her friends; was it somewhere she had yet to discover in the great world beyond?

She would spend hours sitting on the concrete steps in front of her house, surrounded by a garden; home of a little ornamental maple and some lily of the valley, watching a bee tunnel into the mountain of earth that was his home or an ant wander through the landscape of miniature plants. Other days she would sit on a curb in the hot sun, scooping the molten tar with a Popsicle stick from the cracks in the concrete street, lost in another time and space.

She always went to the same place, the memories of long summers spent with her grandmother in a cottage by the woods and the sea. There she felt somehow closer. Could it be hidden in the forest where she would build secret forts, surrounded by ferns and mossy logs sprinkled with sunlight? Or maybe it was in the wind that carried the wonderful smell of the beach with its old, weathered logs and tide pools, where the crabs and fish hid among the rocks and seaweed? Was it in the sky beyond the clouds?

She would look for hours, lying on her back in the dried grass and

CONTINUED ON NEXT PAGE

wildflowers, listening to the cry of the gulls and the chorus of birds hidden in the woods, and sometimes the call of an eagle (which always reminded her of the swing as it swayed back and forth, metal rings squeaking against the wood frame).

She felt at home in the cottage, waking in the morning to the smell of wood smoke, sitting on the fire stool and gazing into the burning embers. Sometimes she would get up in early dawn, pull down the small rowboat, and row out to the reef where there were always fish enough for breakfast and dinner, or to the creek mouth where there were salmon enough for all the neighbors.

It was simple there, away from the roar of traffic and the scurry of people, far from school and math class (which she could never understand the importance of). How did school relate to the wind and the trees and the sky, the smell of the sea and the perfect precision of nature? What did it have to teach her about what she wanted to know?

There was no time in those long summer days—days marked only by dawn and dusk and the hot sun at midday. So simple and so perfect! Suddenly, filled with her memories, she knew she had found it. A feeling of oneness, of peace and incredible joy welled up inside her, unfolded like a flower and filled her whole being with LOVE.

CONTINUED ON PAGE 147

146

Well, that invited a barrage of hostility, based on age-old horse-handler truisms, to which I answered, "Whatever you think," and slunk out. What is the point of trying to force your understanding on another? We must all find the gift in our own lessons.

There have been many seasoned horse people who have approached my barn in fear and trepidation. Some refuse to enter the paddock, feeling unsafe with a dozen or so large creatures that move at will, sometimes at considerable speed. It's interesting, because I have noticed two distinct horse-people types: those who love, and those who fear. This does not mean one shouldn't employ a healthy sense of attention to one's surroundings. Horses are powerful vehicles, and like driving a car, you should proceed with caution. What I am referring to is a strong distrust, possibly based on earlier bad encounters. But with horses, this distrust simply backfires, and often ends up creating the feared situation.

The horse lovers' approach is one of altruistic fascination. The self is forgotten, and they are lost in communion with the horse. These are the worshippers; horses are their religion, and provide the awe-inspiring inspiration for a richer life. The fearful ones have not yet connected with horses at this level, and seem to view horses more as work, or sports equipment. They read the instructions and are careful not to get hurt.

I used to be very much like the latter group, but now, proximity is everything; a divine encounter, and an encounter with the divine. Horse immersion to me is that ultimate experience. I can happily mingle with a dozen horses, welcoming them to interact at their own discretion or to simply share with me their energy as a group. When I was new at this and not able to understand each nuance, I would cringe when one of them lifted a foot, sure that a kick would follow. Over time I realized how acutely aware they are, able to lift a hind foot and scratch a particular spot behind one ear. They knew precisely where I was in relation to that foot, and in fact, had they

Magic and Liz

"Our possessions are few, but they are essential for immortality:
Connection to God and all his creation; Truth, which means a
snake must not try to pretend he is anything other, and
Fidelity, to all that is good; to all that is God."

—Limited Edition (L.E.)
Speaking for the Herd

LOVE was inside her—it had been there all along, in everything; in her parents, her friends; in the little bugs living in the garden. It was just easier to see it here, in nature, surrounded by the glory of life; in its simplicity, away from the hustle, and the rush and the struggle for achievement.

There was nothing to achieve that she didn't have already. It was so clear in those summers by the sea when she had felt at one with every little bird and every blade of grass and every creature that did so perfectly what it was supposed to. It simply loved.

Suddenly she understood. There was one enormous force of love; it was in the air, in the trees, and all the earth, like a river, flowing everywhere, and all of nature flowed with it. Now she knew it was inside of her as much as it was everywhere else, but she had been too busy looking for it. She had been looking everywhere for the one thing she'd had all along. Looking with her eyes; not knowing that it was her eyes.

Her search was over. She had found LOVE and it would be with her always. It was with her in the wind and the trees and the sea and the sky, and in every creature and in every man. She saw them all through her eyes, and her eyes were filled with LOVE.

wanted to dominate me, they could have moved me with a casual blunder forward, or an "I didn't realize you were there" maneuver.

I discovered they were masters at this when I started Parelli. "Oh, excuse me—did I step in your circle and make you move your feet?" Prima would say, using skillful body language. It was a game to her, and she taught me to read her language well. I remember her pleasure when at last I won the game. Horses are comfortable when they have established a leader and no longer need to play the challenge game.

I watched the herd and how they all bowed to L.E.s' will. She was a master, and needed only a subtle look and a particular set of her body to accomplish her will. Not even my little Diva, a most adept street fighter, would even consider another option, and I never saw L.E. do more than just hint at what she might do. It seemed that the middle mares, Diva and Mira, and some of the younger ones like Winnie and Luxy, had to work hard to maintain or advance their order in the herd, while L.E. effortlessly remained the undisputed leader.

I watched L.E. and began to train like she did. Just a glance at a horse's shoulder or hind quarter would move it, but there had to be a certain tip to the head, a concentration of focus that was unmistakably clear. We often play a game called "Stick-to-me." I am the benevolent leader and treat dispenser, as this game is meant to be fun and based on positive reinforcement, a human adaptation of horse language. Treats can take the form of food, scratches, or effusive compliments, and serve as an opportunity for one-on-one companionship. The horses love this game, and line up to go with me, or even approach me at an opportune time and ask for it. A crook of my finger and eye contact with the particular horse and off we go, usually at a run to get out the gate before the others try to follow. I have to quickly close the gate behind us, or I'd have two or three horses fighting to be the only one to play the game with me.

We walk together to the adventure playground, and accomplish various tasks that are difficult and scary for the horse. There are wooden bridges to walk across, plastic swim noodles strung between trees to walk through, logs to jump over, tarps to walk on, and tires, both small and large, to climb up on.

The purpose of the game is to lead the horse happily away from the herd without any mechanical aids, so that it's all their choice, and teach them to watch my body language and depend on me. It always amazes me how much

"Patience" — painting by the author

"White Light" — painting by the author

"Guardian Angel" — painting by the author

more quickly they do things for positive reward, rather than threat of punishment. They have developed a curious and happy attitude, knowing that they are free to participate or not. I am always careful not to stretch their limits to the point where they run back to the herd. I give them time to think about it, or maybe run back a short way if spooked, and then encourage them again. I believe this develops their capacity to reason out situations and trust my judgment rather than just acting blindly in a fearful situation. In the end, they will jump much higher out of love and trust than fear.

Magic, at a year old, had the hardest time with these challenges. Like her mother Diva (and most horses), she had an innate discomfort when it came to stepping on things. I had to use a halter to coax her to step on to the wooden bridge (similar to a mock bridge, it's just eight inches off the ground) for the first time. It took lots of horse treats, but soon, her confidence grew. I remember watching her one day after our session, when the herd was grazing in the playground. Magic showed off her newfound strength by walking to the center of the bridge and stopping, waiting until the whole herd had noticed her. Then, to upstage her, first Picasso and then Matisse ran back and forth over the bridge.

Magic

Picasso at seven months decided he would solicit a stick-to-me game with D.J., my friend Nikki's seven-year-old son. D.J. caught on very quickly and would run circles in the snow, Picasso cantering after him or screeching to a halt when he stopped and moving every part quickly away when advanced upon. Picasso had taught D.J. the game! It was a wonderful sight, watching the two youngsters play as friends.

The babies are the most easily taught. They are very open to cooperating and exploring new activities. It seemed the older horses took a bit longer to process this new relationship. Where before they'd always been led to the ring, now they were invited. There was healthy skepticism to be overcome, as they had already experienced the common aids of bit and crop and the repetitive boring work in the ring. They had to be sold on this new form of play that soon became as enjoyable for them as it did for me. I found if it was interspersed with more traditional training, they still remained willing and happy. "End on a happy note," trainers always said—meaning, quit before the horse refuses and has a tantrum. We would end with some fun games, and then they would freely follow me back to the barn for their big reward of an apple and a carrot.

> I have learned that if not too stressed by a new exercise, a horse will always be won over by a pleasant meal. In a human situation, this would translate to either forcing you onto a porch with a big whip, or offering a glass of wine, some hors d'oeuvres, and a comfortable chair in the sun.

Everyone knows the rules. I say to my horses of choice (of which there might be two or three), "Who wants to come with Mom?" and generally the horses decide. I remember previous times when I would go out with a halter and lead, and whoever I wanted would run away. This didn't happen anymore; now, I give them the choice and make it fun, and they want to play with me. I always feel bad, however, when three accept my invitation and I have to tell two of them, "I still love you, but Prima asked first."

Outside the paddock in my horse-free zone, I have several appealing horse options. One is the hay shed, which offers two choices of neatly stacked hay, one with alfalfa and one with grass. The horses bid on who will be chosen for a visit to this special buffet. They don't so much line up at the gate as quietly approach me while I'm grooming or doing something in the paddock, and sort of whisper in my ear. They place themselves in an obvious position, and send me their thought. (This equates to an expressive look and a raised eyebrow from a close human friend.)

Occasionally, I take the hint and invite them out to the no-horse zone. Of course, they know this involves an invitation to the horse buffet, and they stroll over for nibbles on selected bales. I usually leave them to this special treat for ten minutes or so; then I might offer them another selection from the neighboring vegetable garden. Depending on what's ready at the time, they can choose carrots, beets, peapods, or at the end of the summer, corn stock or cobs.

One funny episode involved Winnie, who voraciously grabbed a whole stalk, and then not wanting to let it go, began to run away from the "scary monster" that was following close behind her head, making rustling noises. She gyrated around several times, increasing the noise as she went, then ran back to the gate and the safety of the herd, still not wanting to let go of the tasty treat. I let her back in and she ran in circles, spooking the entire herd, except

Epona at the adventure playground

ONE WITH THE HERD

Winning Edition (Winnie) age 2, at the adventure playground

I am dreaming: I am in a living room with some people. A large brown thing comes to the door; this is best described as a person in a very large dog suit long floppy ears, plush fur. It runs through the crowd and straight to me, pushes me back against the couch, and leaps on top of me, licking me all over my face. It really loves me! I wake up laughing and laughing
To find this has indeed happened; a big brown animal spirit has just expressed its adoration for me.

of course, Leo, (who at two years old is absolutely bombproof and pops balloons in his mouth). Leo pulled it away from her and began eating it, while the rest stood watching from a safe corner.

A visit to the horse-free zone always allows the horse special, undivided attention and privilege, and strengthens the relationship between us. We play games and groom, and sometimes I even invite the horse to the front porch for an apple or carrot. Since the horses know this area is usually off-limits, there's a degree of bravery involved in leaving the herd and following me for their reward.

I always play "trailer loading" with the horses so that when necessary, they will be able to load in a stress-free manner. When I first started this exercise, I noticed that the younger the horse, and the more imprinted and handled, the more easily he walked in. I have a two-horse angle haul trailer parked and blocked, so it remains stable, a few feet to one side of the garden. There's a big, open yard between the trailer, the garden, and the hay shed, with the open door of the trailer as one option. I never force them to enter, but simply fill a bucket of grain and treats and place it in the corner hay feeder.

The most self-assured foals, like Picasso and Matisse, would simply walk in, eat the food, and leave when they were finished. Winnie would walk in when it was empty and stand there waiting for the reward. If I had two or three young ones out to play, they would all try to wedge in the trailer together, so I kept it to two at most. This worked well when coercing an older, warier horse. I would bring the mares out with their babies, who would casually walk in the trailer and eat, making Mom feel silly. I have learned that if not too stressed by a new exercise, a horse will always be won over by a pleasant meal. In a human situation, this would translate to either forcing you onto a porch with a big whip, or offering a glass of wine, some hors d'oeuvres, and a comfortable chair in the sun. Why do most people not "get it" when dealing with horses? We are most often polite to people; why are we so rude and arrogant with other creatures?

I noticed that some of my horses, no matter how much I assured

Epona and Prima visiting mom

"Glow of Evening" — painting by the author

them, still had a genetic fear of certain things. Magic, just like Diva, had a strong skepticism of caves, so I coaxed her gently, over several days, with no pressure, to enter the trailer. I would place the grain on the edge of the floor, and move it farther back each time. Then I would just go away and let her take her time. The finale was inviting Matisse, her yearling rival and friend, out at the same time. He walked straight in and barely got a mouthful before Magic pushed him over and stuck her head in the bucket. True to form, once she got over the hump, she would run into the trailer for breakfast.

The other game I sometimes play with my horses (and this has gotten me into a lot of trouble with Kevin, whom my father has now nicknamed "the saint") is to invite them up on the front porch to clip-clop along the hollow-sounding wood. The horses are now very comfortable walking not only over wood, but over cattle guards as well (which consequently have had to be replaced, with gates). They now run over to visit me on the porch whenever they break into the horse-free zone. The zone was so named after Kevin's adamant request that he have one small area in 320 acres for himself. (I thought this was unbelievably antisocial of him.) They sometimes visit in the middle of the night, and we wake to multiple clunking sounds and nose prints on the windows.

One morning I got my biggest scare: I had just gotten out of the shower. Looking across the living room at the sliding-glass door, I could see only black. I quickly realized it was Pearl, the Perchie, adoring herself in the mirror of the glass. I realized then the potential for disaster, and quickly stopped Pearl from coming right through the door to visit. The porch still has a bit of a dint on one board from 2,000 pounds of Perchie.

It is always wonderful to watch each new baby explore the world. The other horses line up along the fence, and all try to meet the newborn. I know the herd is ready to rejoin each other when the mare lets down her guard and allows her baby to interact with them.

My other porch-distressing episode involved Epona, who would be very comfortable in the living room if I invited her in. Epona is relaxed enough to sleep on the porch with her nose resting on the window so she can see me inside. For a while, she had to have front shoes put on, after she hurt her hoof. So as she strolled around the porch, checking windows to see where I was, I didn't notice until later that she had left behind permanent horseshoe patterns embossed on the wood. Epona had been good enough to evenly distribute them, however, as well as generously marking the stairs, both up and down.

Always having had a fantasy of living with my horses, I've tried to coerce Kevin into designing me a horse-friendly home. I have talked grates, or sawdust on the floors (imagine—no vacuuming!), but we are still working on the ideal plan. My latest idea was perhaps to have a miniature horse, who could sleep with us as well. (Apparently they wear little running shoes and are housetrained.) Anyway, to date we remain at an impasse, but as long as I spend as much time grooming and playing with Kevin as I do the horses, I am hoping the idea is still on the table.

It is comforting to know that just like Monty Roberts's horse, Shy Boy, the few times my horses have managed to break into the other horse-free zone—which extends for 30 miles or so in either direction—they have

Mira and Matisse

chosen to return. I had reports from the neighboring rancher (who flies over his land) of them grazing miles away, and was wondering how I would ever get them back. I was needlessly panicked. They simply rotated on a larger scale, leaving in the afternoon and returning at six the next morning to their paddock for breakfast.

I have now had five years living as one of the herd on Gateway. The horse operation has had many refinements. We have added a barn help (or horse concierge) house on a hill that we call, simply, Hill House, located behind the Gatehouse. It is a two-story ranch house with a wraparound porch and a lovely view over Kullagh Lake. A hundred yards away is the wall tent which acts as a guest cabin, or an extra storage facility. Our original barn now has an additional large, covered hay shed with a loft overlooking our new birthing stall, which opens onto its own paddock. When the babies are born I can rotate them from the small paddock, which I keep them in for the first day or two (depending on the weather), to the larger 2-acre paddock, by opening a rail gate. At night I move them back to the small paddock so they can easily reach their straw-covered stall. After a couple of weeks, when the baby is strong, I open the rails to the big paddock and barn, and the 10-acre pasture with the lake.

It is always wonderful to watch each new baby explore the world. The other horses line up along the fence, and all try to meet the newborn. I know the herd is ready to rejoin each other when the mare lets down her guard and allows her baby to interact with them. I then introduce a few at a time into the large pasture. The horses make the ultimate decision, when they know their baby is safe, so over the years I have had several break-ins or break-outs. Either the horses on the outside swim across the lake—actually, they wade, as it's not very deep—and get welcomed (or told to stand in the corner), or the new mom, with baby in tow, wades out across the lake. Last year Prima and Picasso lasted in the large pasture about three minutes, as they made a beeline to introduce Picasso to his grandmother, L.E., knowing that under her care the others would keep a respectful distance.

It is always a joy to watch L.E. introduce her babies. She will run with the herd, and there will be an invisible barrier of about fifteen feet around the baby. Who needs a fence when you have such an aura?

SEA OF LOVE

Floating, weightless
In a sea of love,

I have no boundaries,
Within and without

An indescribable joy,
Flows to the eternal reaches of my
soul.

All that I am,
The simple truth,
I now remember.

And wanting never to forget,

Once again I flounder
Like a fish on shore.

Yet the memory lingers
And I want always
To return to the sea.

"Glory" — painting by author

Chapter 10

Glory
HORSE LIFE

GLORY

". . . the special clumsy beauty of this particular colt on this April day, in this field, under these clouds is a holiness consecrated to God, by his own creative wisdom and it declares the glory of God."

—THOMAS MERTON

I ALWAYS LOVE TO WATCH MY HORSES WITH GUESTS, particularly children. Because the horses have always been treated with affection, they are generous in returning it. Cars always catch their interest, and they will line up at the gate to visit with guests. I have to warn visitors that a backside presented to them is not a slight but an invitation for mutual bonding. It can be disconcerting to some people when several large horses surround them, but they are just curious and outgoing. If a project is under way, they will surround heavy equipment or workers with chain saws or hammers, and rest their heads on shoulders and genuinely try to help out.

I remember when we received some dump-truck loads of gravel for the paddock. As soon as one would unload a pile, the horses would fight for the title of "King of the Castle." Whenever there's any kind of pile in the paddock, it will be claimed as the perfect sunbathing spot. The horses love parties. Particularly amusing was tobogganing one winter with all the children and grandchildren, down the hill at the end of the foal pasture. The horses were fascinated, and when the toboggans were pulled up the hill they would all advance. The minute someone came down they would all run back to the barn. This went on for an hour or so, and when we were all finished, the horses ran up and down the track several times to see if it was as fun as it looked. (Kevin was thrilled at the deep footprints all over his carefully manicured run.)

I have speakers in the barn, so the horses can enjoy the music and the party mood. They get very excited and run around the pasture to entertain us when we are sitting out on the porch. I can really get them going if I start a game of tag or chase them with my Indian war cry, "Yiiiaaahooo!!"

The most wonderful thing to watch, though, is how gentle and careful they are with children. The smaller the child, the lower they drop their heads. My grandchildren kiss them on the nose, and they hold their heads so still to receive the honor. I have put children (whose legs barely extend over the seat of the saddle) on Diva, and have asked her to help them, and with simple word commands, she will walk on, trot, whoa, and back up. I really do believe that the more trust you place in a horse, the more she will reward you with integrity.

The other way the horses show their kindness is to small animals. I remember when we got our new kitten, Noon. He loved the barn and the horses, and at just two months old, this little fluff ball would wind his way between legs and lie amid feet, while three or four horses stroked him with their noses, blowing gently and making him purr wildly.

In the nice weather, Noon will blast out of the woods and run along the pasture fence to the paddock at about thirty miles an hour. It's amazing to see how discerning these prey animals are. They don't bat an eyelash if our cats or dogs appear out of nowhere at a fast run, or if I jump around and do any number of silly things, but should a coyote or deer, or even an unknown human, walk across a hill, unseen to us except through binoculars, all eyes and ears are directed toward the interloper. This is the same for unknown visitors in cars. However, when I return from somewhere, even in a friend's car, I get just a casual glance of identification before they all resume eating. How do they know it's me, a mile away inside a car?

One day, I found the herd in the hills, all surrounding a large rock, their attention fixed on whatever was underneath it. I walked over to investigate, and found a scared little marmot on his back with his feet in the air, attempting to hold back these giants. The horses were snorting gently like they sometimes do to their babies. They meant him no harm, but I couldn't coax them

Granddaughter Kaia and L.E.

"You can lead a horse to water, but you can't make him drink.

You can lead a man to pasture, but you can't make him eat."

—PremiereEdition (Prima)
Speaking for the Herd

away. Luckily the marmot had a strong heart and was perfectly fine once the horses finally wandered away.

As I've mentioned, I have the reputation among most of my friends of being a little on the fringe. I quite commonly make reference to my conversations with horses, which can be had from any distance, and if I'm confused or worried about what I'm getting, or not getting, I will call an animal communicator for a second opinion. I also do healing and employ healers in the same way. I believe all minds are joined, and everything can be solved on the spiritual level.

Leo

"The thing I like most, is the warm feeling I get when I am around other people or animals that make me feel loved. I have always felt safe and comforted."

— Leonardo (Leo)
Speaking for the Herd

I remember when Diva lost her twins, she was depressed for about three months, and angry at some of the other horses, especially Prima, who was ten months pregnant at the time. Whenever Diva would see me, she would nicker, like she did to her babies, and then she'd ferociously guard me from the rest of the herd. She didn't understand what had happened with her babies even though I had explained it to her over and over. Just like a grieving human, she didn't want to believe her babies were dead. I was getting increasingly worried, as she had chased a very pregnant Prima through and over fences, and talking to her was like reasoning with a jealous sibling. Diva had always been my little nature spirit. Although her full name is "Divine Edition," I made the mistake of shortening it. You have to be careful in the name you choose. Anyway, I finally called an animal communicator friend and asked her to talk to Diva.

The next morning we awoke to a new Diva: ears forward, eyes bright, the weight had been lifted. It was something she couldn't talk about with me. She was depressed thinking that she had killed her first baby, and she believed that I hadn't trusted her with the second. She was also jealous of Prima, whom she thought I loved more, and who was going to have a baby when she couldn't. She wondered why I'd believed that I could care for her baby better than she could? I ask myself the same question.

Diva now has her filly, Magic, and adores her. At a year and a half, Magic is never away from her mom, and her every whim is generously answered. Rather than spoiling her as it would a human baby, this has made her very outgoing and secure. I have been telling Magic that her mom will have a little sister this year, and she is excited to help care for her.

Knowing how close my horses are to their families, I find it difficult to accept how the majority of people treat their mares. We all know farms that employ unthinkable methods, and are morally depraved. I won't say any more about them. However, even the average well-run breeding farm, with caring owners, follows the generally accepted practice of weaning at four to six months. They remove a terrified baby from its mother, locking both far away from each other, never to be reunited. I think this is barbaric, and the sad thing is, there is no empathy for the horses. People convince themselves that it's acceptable to do terrible things for money; the majority doesn't believe animals should be acknowledged as having any feelings, let alone rights.

My focus is on finding perfect families for my babies; at the right time, when mare and baby are ready and the right person appears, I let the mothers decide when it's time to wean. I have had mares like Millie who just don't want to give their babies up. When Mira aborted last year, she continued to nurse

Matisse until a few months ago, as she is bred for this year. He is about a hand bigger than she is right now, and it looks very funny watching a baby bend its knees to nurse, but I have not found it to be detrimental in any way to the mare, and the baby is far more emotionally secure for it.

In the wild, mothers normally wean when the next baby is due, or if not bred, by around age two. They used to encourage human mothers to wean early, and now many mothers are nursing until age two, or even three. It is a loving, nurturing thing to do, and the only problem with horses is, it gets in the way of the demands we make on them. I continue to ride my nursing moms and either take the baby with us, or come back after an hour or so to allow them to nurse. Prima is still nursing Picasso (at age two); her udder has shrunk, so I can take her away for hours, but when we return, they are right back together. I just laugh!

Even when the next baby is born, the families stay together. They wander with the herd in order: Mom, new baby, and then in order of age, last baby, and baby before that. The older children often babysit, play, and groom the younger ones. I remember when Mira had Leo, it was Luxy who would run back and get him if Mira (who is a pretty relaxed mom) would wander off when he was sleeping. Leo now looks after Matisse, his younger brother, teaching him all the boy games, and Matisse (who as yet doesn't have a younger sibling) has adopted Picasso, passing his knowledge down to him. The families stand in their groups in the barn and groom each other, and will generally all stand around the younger ones as they sleep—or at least lie in close proximity.

The other morning, Suzanna, our horse concierge, climbed down the ladder to find Magic sprawled next to Picasso, her head on his chest, and L.E. sound asleep in doggie position, her chin resting on the sawdust. L.E. was dreaming, nickering to her soon-to-be-born baby. Suddenly, she let out a huge whinny in her sleep. I suppose the baby must have run off!

Spring is rapidly approaching, and birthing days, clearly marked on our horse calendars, are drawing near. Daily I check my mares for any signs of bagging up (milk in the udder), softening of the muscles and ligaments in the hind end, and that telltale sign of imminent birth, waxing. This is when the wax plugs in the teats are forced out by the pressure of the milk.

By spring we are expecting five new babies—a first for us, as we usually

Prima and Picasso

"We are all one, Human, Plant, Animal, Rock. — Every single little quark is united in the same cosmic soup. There are spaces but no boundaries. Boundaries are only thoughts."

—Premiere Edition (Prima)
Speaking for the Herd

have only one or two. I know my mares really appreciate the help, and I know how dangerous birthing can be, so I drag my sleeping bag to the birthing stall and maintain my vigil there until the baby appears. I get a few short bits of sleep, but I am awake at the slightest noise; the pacing, the getting up and down, and the water breaking, anxiously awaiting that first little foot. My mares usually

ONE WITH THE HERD　　　**171**

come and stand over me to wake me up just before the water breaks.

My babies are extremely large, being Warmbloods with 17- to 17.2-hand fathers. Very often I will give a tug at the right moment, or make sure they are aligned and then pull with each contraction. I rip open the sack when the baby is presented, make sure they're breathing, and then towel-dry them off. Usually at this point, the mother is helping me by licking as fast as I am drying. I am kissing and hugging my mare through this whole process, and telling her what a good job she's doing. I know they love the help and the attention. This also makes for very gregarious babies when they enter the world to a welcoming committee and a lot of love. I often will have a friend or two who want to see a birth. Trudy, my friend, art agent, and Matisse's other, other, mom, was there for his birth, and Matisse was sucking her fingers before his mother's teat. To this day he loves and welcomes her whenever she comes to visit.

I don't so much "imprint" as welcome the babies to the world. I share in the absolute joy of birth, camping out with the new family, until the baby is nursing regularly and relaxing comfortably while I stroke and hold them. I give the mothers a nice warm meal and freshen the straw for their cozy bed. I remember Leo was particularly large and slow to nurse. He actually was drinking out of the cup I used to catch the colostrum, before he managed a teat, which I had to position in the cup until he got the idea. He would, however, manage to place himself so that when he lay down, his head would rest on my pillow. (I had to get an extra one for myself.)

Today, Leo—at 17.2 hands and almost three years old (Warmbloods grow until they're six)—lumbers after me to the playground. If we play tag, I can't lose him, hiding behind trees and bushes. He is absolutely bombproof and curious about everything he sees. I am sure his self-assuredness had its roots in that early time we spent together.

Ultimately, the first time I put a saddle on their backs, my babies are unimpressed, and equally so when I sit on them. From the time they are born and sleeping in the barn, I will lie on top of them and snuggle, or underneath them, cradling their heads; we are completely comfortable together.

Sometimes when starting my young horses, I will put someone else on them, and the horse will follow me around the ring while the rider gives the signals. This usually works best, for if I'm on top, my babies turn around and look at me or talk to my foot, asking for instruction. This tendency for reassurance from above, however, works very well in Level 2 Parelli, when you take the bridle on and off from the horse's back. My guys are quite content to parley with my foot for extended periods, giving me time to complete the task.

I have bred to some very impressive sires. Lynx, who is the father of Prima, Luxy, Leo, Magic, and Matisse, is the black stallion that dreams are made of. A 17.2-hand Holsteiner with amazing bloodlines, he has a fabulous jump and is distinguished in dressage. He won the lifetime achievement award from the Canadian Warmblood Horse Breeders Association. Kingston, Epona's sire, is a young stallion who was reserve champion at his licensing and has sired several premium babies and performance champions. This year I have bred to Pacific Star and Sandstorm, two first premium Dutch Warmbloods at their licensing. Sandstorm is a tricolor pinto, and I am very excited about this addition to my herd. L.E. and Winnie are having Sandstorm babies. Picasso's sire is Fabriano, a Hanoverian who is a Furioso son. Luxy is bred to him as well for this year. Having raised six children of my own, I can now vicariously enjoy motherhood with my four-legged babies.

It is a lot easier to determine genetics in horses than humans. Our foals are not only stunningly beautiful, but they have wonderful minds as well. Good beginnings, careful handling, clear communication, and lots of love have produced carefree, willing partners who can begin life without the scars so often apparent in babies who are not as fortunate.

My ongoing worry is in finding them homes that will offer them, if not the same quality of surroundings or space, at least the same respect and consideration they receive here at Gateway. I look for fellow horse worshippers, and I believe they are growing in numbers, as the voice of animals is starting to be heard. There are those out there who believe that the glory of God is expressed in myriad ways, and not just in the privilege of being human. They extend common courtesy and affection to all creatures, regardless of language, color, shape, or breed.

I have noticed another interesting development recently. Normally in horse-human relationships, there are horse laws and human laws. Living in such close proximity, it seems we have developed horse-human agreements or laws that are mutually brought forth and respected. The birthing stall, for instance, supercedes any predetermined hierarchy in the herd. When a horse approaches me and asks for the birthing stall, it comes with diplomatic immunity to all other laws. The horses respect this. When a soon-to-be mother is in protective custody of the birthing stall, superior members of the herd respect the rights that are afforded such a position.

I watch as Winnie, one of the youngest mares (and therefore, one of the lowest in the pecking order), waits in the birthing stall short moments before her indoctrination into motherhood. Diva approaches and asks for acceptance. An older and significantly superior mare, she wishes to confer with Winnie about the situation, and because Winnie is in a position of honor bestowed by me (i.e., in possession of the birthing stall), Diva asks for permission to speak to her. Luxy, her direct superior by one year (but also her friend), comes to the fence and asks if she can drink from the birthing stall water. Luxy is waiting to birth next and respects the order we have established. Birthing horses get the stall and all privileges associated with it: food, water, treats, massage, and undivided attention.

The horse whose time is near will approach me, drop her head, and send a picture of the blessed event, to which I respond hurriedly, and the two of us run to the birthing stall together, to spend a few hours preparing for the celebration. The rest of the herd—those in the inner circle (mares about to birth) who are in the foal paddock and main barn area, and the "outcasts" (youngsters and unbred mares—who are loose on the 320 acres and have a connecting paddock so they can feel included)—will not leave the immediate area. Birth is about to begin.

This year, although I now wonder what possessed me, I bred five mares. Mira kept April (my friend and Luxy's human mom) and me sleeping in the loft above the stall for only four or five days. In her usual manner, Mira quickly and efficiently gave birth to a Goliath of a baby boy, Miro. A strong, big-boned bay with three socks and a blaze, he is the firstborn of the new batch of foals.

Diva, on the other hand, kept us awake and attentive for a week, trying to position Serene for birth. Serene was another darker bay with three socks and a star. Diva believes birth is difficult, and manages to have one tense situation after another. This year she birthed around midday to an audience made up of Kevin, Clive, April, and me. We became seriously concerned, as the baby was positioned sideways and slightly upside down. I called the vet, who, despite being forty-five minutes away, still showed up to save the day during the final few seconds of both their lives. Diva was contracting, trying to push an intractable baby out of the birth canal and managing to almost prolapse her intestine while doing it. "Serene" entered the world as anything but serene — in shock and not breathing. We all rallied, and April saved her by giving the near-dead baby artificial respiration. We were not about to let her die, and the vet was amazed at our determination and manifestation skills. Serene is now a healthy, beautiful two-month-old, romping in the meadow with her foal friends, or lying quietly while visitors exclaim about how her coat feels like plush fur to the touch.

> The horse whose time is near will approach me, drop her head, and send a picture of the blessed event, to which I respond hurriedly, and the two of us run to the birthing stall together, to spend a few hours preparing for the celebration.

Following Serene's birth, we spent two and a half weeks waiting for a very overdue Winnie and Luxy (both giving birth to their first foals), never certain how imminent the births actually were. At last they decided to get it over with on the same night: Winnie gave birth to Monet, a perfect, good-sized pinto, at 10:30 P.M., and Luxy followed suit at 2:30 A.M. with Max, another pinto. We were amazed, because Luxy hadn't been bred to a pinto, and it was a stray Sabino gene that caused the unexpected alteration. (A Sabino gene is one that is commonly responsible for all socks and blazes on horses, but taken to a more extreme level, it will express itself in pinto markings.) Little Max was certainly unique, being able to walk under his 17-hand mother. Babies are always a surprise!

The funniest incident was with Winnie, who after birthing, rose and looked out the half wall of the birthing stall. She began greeting the mares who were waiting to see the event. She must have thought that she'd just had a bad stomachache, because she seemed to have no idea that her baby was patiently waiting for some attention. We directed Winnie to the wet little lump, and the look of shock on her face was hysterical as she proceeded to lick, nuzzle, and nicker over and over in disbelief. She has remained a wonderful and patient mother.

Last of all was L.E. We were praying she would have a girl to replace the baby she'd lost the year before. Miraculously, not only was the new foal a girl, but also a perfect duplicate of the lost foal, right down to the same star-shaped mark on her forehead. Crystal is so like her mother, and perfect in every way.

The babies are now quite the herd of gregarious, curious, and adorable little beings, flocking around visitors, begging for a scratch or a little grooming.

My friends Mike and Mardi visited for a week with their children, Rylan (eleven), Griffin (seven), and Aria (five). Both sets of young ones immediately struck up a friendship, the children hugging, cuddling, and playing with all of the horses, but having a particular affinity with the babies. They communicated freely, telling me what Crystal or Serene had said, and fearlessly sticking their fingers into the babies' mouths to see how hard they would bite (not hard) and testing to see who hugged back the best. The horses loved the whole family, as they were so spontaneous, intuitive, and loving. The babies would run to play with the children and the whole herd would return three times a day to visit, following their car back to the guesthouse. Matisse, who had fallen hopelessly in love with Mardi, stood guard at night by her front door.

Two years old and barely ridden, one morning Matisse just wouldn't leave Mardi alone. She was sitting on the paddock fence and Matisse kept walking up to her and saying "Get on!" Mardi asked what I thought of this idea, and I told her his status: very green, no tack, probably not a great idea, especially since Mardi was a novice rider. Matisse, however, had other ideas, and he coerced her into putting a leg over his back. When that was accomplished, he slid underneath and walked off with his prize. He then very proudly paraded around the paddock for about ten minutes, stopping for an apple and to pose for some pictures. I find it surprising how quickly doorways open when everyone is communicating.

Aria and babies

"Larger than Life"— painting by the author

When I learned that John Lyons had lost his longtime best friend, "Bright Zip" I deeply felt his loss knowing how much I loved my horses, so I had to do this painting for him.

Larger Than Life
THE SPIRITUAL INTERFACE

Many years ago I looked in a baby name book to see the meaning of my given names. Elizabeth means "oath of God," and Ann means "grace." After some reflection on my life's purpose, I channeled the following, recording it in my journal:

> Elizabeth, oath of God, lost human, who are
> you. And what have you come to do? Paint, that
> is a definite, love animals; the pieces
> of the puzzle are all in place, but how do
> they fit? Where are the clear signs? What
> can I do to extend God's grace, to become
> that grace? Fears are still holding me back.
> TRUST, TRUST, TRUST. I am given that
> over and over. Am I just drifting, or is there
> a direction that is still unclear? I have a
> vague recollection that I must do something—
> but what? Is it inherent? Will I do it
> no matter what, or must I remember? I
> want guidance; I need a clear vision.—
> "Elizabeth, this is a sacred exercise
> between you and God. The point of a

BEGINNING TO KNOW

I am beginning to know that God's truth is present in each moment. Nothing is ever wrong; it just appears so from our perspective. The more we know this in our hearts, the more it is manifested in our reality.

There is no cause for concern. It is all perfect and as it should be. Just as the seasons from the viewpoint of a whole cycle are necessary and perfect in their individual and distinct character, so is the succession of our days, when viewed from a larger perspective, each necessary and perfect in their individual variation.

The cloak of Christ or God's peace that the mystics talk about is the foundation of our lives when we surrender to the wisdom and perfection of each circumstance. My experience is unique and perfect for only me. It is orchestrated in infinite detail for my own individual evolution.

Just as a flower seed has all the information to create a particular flower, the seed of God must simply allow itself to grow. By eliminating distraction and trusting in the process, we are allowing growth unhampered by the limitations of our ego.

sacred exercise is just that—exercise.
You think too much. A direction is a
temporary expression. Enjoy it!
You give power by your thoughts.
Remember "looking for love." It is
in your eyes.
   The reality of creation is only that."

Whenever I have needed assurance, my introspection generally appears in the form of an answer that is symbolically perfect, and understood only by me. I was told that as a child, I'd had a wild imagination, and now my friends just refer to me as "flaky." It is interesting to note, however, that more often than not, over time they come to accept my philosophies without question.

I have always had Pegasus as my spirit guide, and he is very present to manipulate day-to-day situations in my favor. He oversees my safety, as at times, my right-brained driving has just about gotten me killed. The other car will take a wide berth, missing me by inches. He is excellent at clearing traffic, finding the ideal parking spot, or carrying me directly to the solution to any problem.

I remember at a spiritual workshop once, I participated in an exercise called "the cube." We were to imagine a cube alone in the desert, and then visualize or make notes about what we saw. Then we would add a ladder, a horse, a storm, and last of all, flowers to the scene. Everyone had a unique version, and I won't spoil it (in case you come across this exercise) by telling you the meaning, but I will describe what I saw:

   My cube was a clear crystal, which changed light into many colors;
   my ladder, a golden curved stairway to heaven; my horse Pegasus to
   take me there, and my storm, an iridescent tornado of white light that
   wrapped me in God's love.

It was interesting because Kevin's cube was bright and golden, and I have always referred to him as the sun in my life, and our flowers were the same, multicolored primroses, evenly spaced everywhere, representing the six children that we share.

Hercules (Hercy)

Pegasus was there to welcome my whippet Hercules when he died, and absolutely bereft, I just had to have him back. I had been told animals often reincarnate and come back to their earth families. I bought dog breed books and breeder guides, and came up with a perfect new body for my little whippet: a Leonberger—bred to look like a lion, gentle, loved children, and a good protector of the home. I found a breeder nearby at Guardian Angel Farms. The following excerpt from my journal tells this story.

Requiem for Hercules

Beloved light being, I was given a synopsis this morning—Herc was a drop of sunlight, like you would see sparkling on the water, or in a drop of dew; beautiful iridescent sunlight. He came into our lives when I was chanting: I am an unlimited God; I embody wisdom, truth, joy, freedom, abundance, and love. Think about it—that was Herc. Joy manifested, — freedom, abundance, and love! He was a lover; he was a joy freak, but we named him Hercules, and he had an insurmountable task to complete. He was tested; his joy too much for this limited plane, and in his last battle with the many-headed monster (several coyotes), he finally reached his goal: "Truth and enlightenment," the angel of which is Ra, also known as the sun god. Very fitting for a spark of sun . . . Herc is coming back as Ra, bred by Guardian Angel dog farms. Herc is shining in my heart, very much with me always, and today I meditated about his coming back, and I get a clear picture of a shining sunburst on the heart of the new puppy.

I phoned the breeder and arranged for a puppy—but now the question was, how to get the right one without her thinking I was crazy. There was a two-month wait, and I was counting the days.

It was early March, and I was doing my morning chores, and suddenly I felt it—Herc was back. I ran to the phone and called the breeder, dragging her away from the birth to tell me the first puppy had been born. I knew it was him. She told me she marked each puppy with a dab of nail polish on their heads, so she could follow their progress. Absolutely unnecessary, as two months later when we were allowed to claim a puppy, sure enough, that was the only one with a white sunburst over the heart. This, however, did not mean all would go smoothly, as a whippet in a Leonberger body is quite the handful!

Ra's outline on the frosty porch. How did a Leonburger leave a whippet outline?

My darling Epona was another example of bringing spirit forth in body. I had just read *The Tao of Equus*, and so wanted a horse goddess in my herd. I asked for Epona, but having bred my dark bay mare to a dark bay sire, I was amazed when the result was a golden girl. As I have mentioned, Epona is a goddess in every way.

The road to spiritual discovery has many pitfalls as well as milestones. It has often been described by saints and sages as a roller-coaster ride. Amazingly, whenever I am in over my head, I have always been thrown a lifeline.

Not long after moving to our home at Gateway, in the quiet of the first long winter, I had asked for a sign that everything was on track. The answer appeared one morning as I went to write in my journal and channeled the following:

Trust me Elizabeth, you are afraid of speed. I know that, and I am gentle with you. All is precisely perfect. Have fun, be joy-full; be free. The world is a big adventure. Dream your dreams, and ask me to manifest them. You've seen how quickly I work. Try me again and again; ask the seemingly impossible. I will give it to you in the blink of an eye.

Test me; I love tests. Don't you realize that since we are one, the love you feel for me is my love for you. The fact that you are here now, means that I have met all your needs until now. As you awaken to the understanding that as a divine being you need nothing, you will experience more and more, becoming what you know yourself to be.

Then later that morning, standing in the paddock, surrounded by my beloved horses, I got yet another confirmation. Suddenly there appeared in the distant sky a multicolored UFO, which, after drifting closer and closer, descended into the paddock. It was in fact a large bouquet of helium balloons, with a note that read CONGRATULATIONS! YOU HAVE WON THE SHOOT-ING STAR AWARD.

This was all the more amazing because we were miles from the nearest town. And I had been complaining that life seemed to be unfolding too slow-ly! The award was from a store called Hollywood Video, and upon doing a lit-tle research, I discovered that the nearest one is located 120 miles away, in a little town called Hope.

I wrote earlier of healing creatures. I have always maintained health in my family. I believe that first, the spiritual is manifest (as a thought form—an idea in the mind of God), and the physical form follows that etheric template, which is an energetic blueprint, an electromagnetic template that holds the form into which physical matter flows. At the simplest level, if one holds to the spiritual truth of perfection, clearly, and in complete faith, physical perfection will follow suit. I call this God's truth in all life, and it is always perfection. When I am faced with any form of illusion, which is served in large portions on the physical plane, I simply hold to that idea of God's perfection, and all else disappears.

This continues to amaze me every time it happens, but I have witnessed many of what must be termed "miracles." One of the most impressive was

Diva's first baby, Michelangelo, a beautiful black bay colt, my second foal. From my journal:

> *Michelangelo showed up one morning unable to put any weight on his foreleg. The vet was sure it was broken at the shoulder, and wanted to move him to Vancouver for extensive testing, X-rays, surgery, pins, and plates; or, maybe I should just put him down now and save a lot of money. Wow, that was certainly a big lump of illusion!*
>
> *I didn't sleep all night. Everyone went to Stump Lake for the weekend, and I stayed home. Hands-on healing, visualization, homeopathy, and affirmations. Three days later, he was galloping around the pasture. Interesting that it was his shoulder, and a few days earlier I awoke in the morning with a sore shoulder. Alex called and gave me affirmations from **Heal Your Life** by Louise Hay: "I easily flow with change and new experience. My life is divinely guided, always going in the right direction . . ." "I experience life as a joyous dance."*

I have since had other horse miracles. Leo and Matisse, brothers and enormous babies out of Mira, had contracted tendons and clubfeet. The vets insisted on surgery, which I refused, and at ages two and three, they are both perfect today, with no intervention but my request for a miracle and some natural healing.

One of the strangest signs that both Kevin and I experienced occurred on the day before September 11, 2001. Kevin had just returned home from a trip to Kamloops, and we both looked at each other and said, "You won't believe what happened today." Kevin's story first: He was driving along a lonely strip of road and was arrested by the striking visual image of a dead black dog lying at the foot of a memorial wreath. He was then tailgated by two cars for the rest of the trip, which is about twenty miles, and they never varied in their position. Suddenly, just before our driveway, they both disappeared. There was no turnoff in sight, and he'd sat there waiting for them to pass, not quite believing the strange feeling he had.

My story is that I was in the kitchen, and drips of red began to appear on the counter. On the shelf above, there was a plastic food coloring container split in half for no reason. Then bang-bang, against the window, two identical birds hit. I ran out to hold them upright and save them, but they were both stone dead. I always save birds when they hit the window, but that might be one or two a year. The next day we heard about the suicide bombers.

So now I will explain my theory, and the title to this chapter, "Larger than Life."

Larger, of course, means more visible. The visibility of the spiritual realm of life is, I believe, a gift that horses bring to us. Being empathic creatures, and living as all animals do, at the crossroads of the spiritual and the physical worlds, they interact with our higher spiritual selves. When we spend time in their presence, we open to their world. As I wrote before, it's like being immersed in a foreign culture. After time we absorb the language and the customs. Immersion in HORSE leads to communication and understanding in the spiritual realm. We grow comfortable in their world, a world of crystalline insight, where pictures and feelings flash clearly across MIND and MIND is a timeless connection to a higher truth (meaning Universal Mind,) to which we are all connected.

Beyond the dimension that is known to the ego lies the simple truth that is clearly obvious to animals, and equally obscure to us humans:

We are all one with God, and God is all there is: relax and enjoy the experience.

Michaelangelo, age 2

"Animals interconnect, species-to-species to man, — and that is how we can help you."

—PremiereEdition (Prima)
Speaking for the Herd

Solitaire
AT ONE WITH THE EARTH

SOLITAIRE

*Sometimes for an instant
when I catch your eye,
I know the truth.
It's like a masquerade,
and we are both pretending to
play people,
and pretending to be fooled.
I know who you really are,
and why I'm here.
And when for an instant,
your mask slips away,
I know it's all a farce.
There is only one game, and one
player
and all that matters is to learn the
rules.*

Although our property itself is parklike, with groves of trees and surrounding meadows and lakes, it still needs stewardship to maintain its health. These are dry grasslands, and although the forests are advancing, and healthy little fir trees dot our meadows, winters are getting milder and snow-fed lakes are diminishing. Being dependent on wind or solar energy, we carefully plan ahead for projects that require energy.

Water has been an ongoing concern. Although we have a good well, and plenty of softened, filtered, and even re-energized water for our barn and home, we have tried unsuccessfully to drill wells at other locations. The Gatehouse and Hill House share a water source that is meager at best, so we have holding tanks that can be filled by a water truck. Although water witches told us there's plenty of water below the surface, it is comparable to the tar sands and is difficult to access. The grass there stays green all summer, but there is not a clear flow.

This year our project is to help fill the lake in the foal pasture, as it has dwindled over the past few years. It is a constant solace for us, as well as the horses and animals living in this area.

There is also yearly pasture maintenance, and early each spring we weed, harrow, clean up winter debris (like fallen branches and stones), and re-seed bare patches. My foal pasture and

"Road Less Travelled," Gateway 2 Ranch — painting by the author

adventure playground get the most attention, as they have to be safe for the babies.

There is a garden to plant, and with the black earth of this area and several years' accumulation of manure, it produces more then enough vegetables, for friends as well. My friend April is our gardener, and she meticulously arranges everything in neat rows, while I tend to scatter my greens a little more loosely. (I figure you buy them as mixed greens for salad anyway.)

The horses are ever helpful in these projects, always there when wells are being dug or tractors appear. They follow all the helpers around, asking politely if they can be of assistance. They particularly love gardening, and line up along the fence to partake of any "thinnings."

The horses cultivate the land in their own way. They have wooded areas where they gather for shade; places where they harvest certain herbs or flowers; soft, deep, grassy places where they sleep; and even some special places for play. I remember when I discovered the babies' play fort. There is a copse of aspen next to their pasture with the view of the lake, and when it's hot in the summer, it offers shade and a small pond to splash in. There is lush green grass, and I go there to be with the horses, and pick dandelions for my salads (if the horses don't extract them from me first). I was happily following my dandelions when I came across a pathway through the trees that led into a magical covered circle. It had been cleared and trampled, and overhead was a type of weeping tree that offered shade and seclusion. It was only tall enough for the babies, and I watched them go there to play and sleep when their moms were grazing nearby.

The horses also love their sphagnum moss bog, which Prima showed me on one of our rides. It's a huge circle of soft, spongy moss, damp beneath, and the horses (along with the deer, moose, and elk) go there to roll and rest in the cool, deep shade of the forest. They have their places for munching on rotten logs, or thistles, and one of their favorite delicacies, rose hips. In the fall when rose hips are everywhere, I love to roam with my herd and help them pick. I am so much better at it, having fingers, and although they watch me closely and try to imitate, I do a much better job. I fill my fleece with at least a quart, and then distribute them to whoever seems the neediest. Again, this is another bonding exercise, and we communicate well; when I just look at the bushes and a particular horse, they know it's their turn.

They seem to know exactly what is needed, and will satisfy their medicinal needs as well. I often see them eating wild garlic, or nibbling on lichens. They have not needed to be wormed since our move here, and I keep checking their stools at the vet's. I still find it hard to believe.

The one silly thing I've watched them do is gnaw on the bark of the aspens at the end of winter, consequently killing the trees. I wondered at the purpose of that, but it was beyond my comprehension. It turns out that like weeds, the aspens are dispensable, and have a fast turnover. Recently I was told by L.E. and Diva that there is something in the bark that keeps ticks and other biting insects away. I always wondered why the older horses didn't suffer

THE GARDEN

"Never have I experienced such immaculate landscape; like a country estate, groomed to perfection, by a loving gardener.
I want to shout to the trees—
I feel your love; your joy,
and I love you back. I will love you forever.
This is, after all, a marriage."

"Homestead" — painting by the author

from the bugs.

There are so many diverse ecosystems on Gateway, from hilltops to valleys, marshes to deserts, and my herd enjoys them all. There is nowhere I have been on the property—and I have walked every square inch—that the horses have not. Every once in a while, one will come in with a cactus on the end of its nose. These are nasty little things, I know, because one time when I was following the herd, I sat down abruptly on a patch of them. I was wearing cutoffs at the time, and as well as embedding themselves in both my hands, they were securely planted in my backside. I didn't know where to begin plucking, and sadly discovered that they have barbs as well. Now when I see a horse with one on the end of its nose, I am very sympathetic. Tick season, which generally runs from the first day of warmth in the spring to the heat of summer, was like a horror movie to me the first time I encountered it.

After the first experience with tweezers and buckets of water (which they promptly climbed out of), I became outraged on behalf of my horses. I now simply pull the ticks off, mutilate them, and flick them to the ground. There are usually only three or four on probably two-thirds of the horses, for about six weeks. Not so bad in the grand scheme of things, but bad enough. I have never found any on the dogs, and only one or two on me. They tickle, and I pull them off immediately. We simply don't picnic during that season, and it's not that serious, as we do not have Lyme disease or Rocky Mountain Spotted Fever here.

I have discovered several natural remedies for horses who are susceptible to ticks. Epona, being blonde, is particularly sensitive to mosquitoes, flies, and ticks. I feed her a product from Cheval International, called Inside Out. It is apple cider vinegar, molasses, and garlic (among other ingredients), and it makes horses unpalatable for insects. I also use fly predators on my manure pile, and that has reduced my pest problem significantly. Now with Radionics (www.taranet.co.uk/radionics.htm), Radionics is "a healing technique in which our natural ESP faculties are used to both discover the energetic disturbances underlying illness, and to encourage the return of a normal energetic field which supports health." You can create a thought form around your house and barn, which flies will not cross. (This is something like in quantum physics, where you get the results you believe in.) I'm not exactly sure how, but it appears to work!

We refuse to use poisons, and that has caused us considerably more work, but we hand-pull knapweed and other noxious weeds, and use natural remedies whenever we can.

Animals walk softly compared to us. We create such a mess from our consumerism and our predatory behavior. There are so many abandoned homesteads in our hills, which have left more than their share of debris. Boards with nails and barbed wire are ubiquitous hazards. I was once riding in the hills and saw a cow wrapped in barbed wire left from a fence. I called the rancher, who had to shoot it. I have removed all the wire on our well-worn routes, but it always makes me wonder how we can be so unconscious of our impact on the earth. Animals do not share our ambitions or our greed. There are so many times I pass idyllic patches of countryside littered with old cars and junk. I wonder if this serves the same purpose as when a squirrel hoards its nuts.

In my case, I am ever-vigilant of unnecessary debris. Kevin and I have almost divorced over this issue several times, as he is a collector and I am a purist. He spreads tools and possible necessities among four locations around our home. The woodshed, the tractor shed, the generator shed, and the top of my barn. It has become my barn, as the horse-free zone has become Kevin's. My last stronghold of order, the top of the barn, was designed for horse use—meaning feed and buckets—and I need access to all of the feed tubes in order to keep everything functioning smoothly. Every once in a while I will crack down, and arrange a massive cleanup and relocation of all the stray tools and paraphernalia that has wandered into my barn, or the uncluttered horse-free zone. I am now lobbying for doors on the tractor shed to obscure the black hole of Kevin's untouchables. This is for his benefit, since the horses might very well eat them.

But beyond the ecologically sensitive issues here, there are large amounts of silence and solitude on Gateway. There are also times that are festive and joyful. This is the gift of polarity: One extreme enables you to appreciate the other, and between the two, you find that middle road.

When we left the Sunshine Coast and our busy home, I remember being told that it doesn't matter where you go, you will simply re-create your truth, your life. In our small community in Gibsons, B.C., raising six children, we had lots of friends. We were almost famous there, Kevin being the town architect, and I the artist and fund-raiser for every nonprofit group in the area. We always had friends visiting us, and many parties to attend. We even had tour buses arriving to see the studio.

Moving to the middle of nowhere, you would think that this lifestyle would end. Obviously, we have re-created here (as in the belief that you will continue to re-create your understanding wherever you go), as on many a weekend, especially in the summer, you will find several cars in our driveway. There is even a tour bus of sorts, as our friend Lorne, who built a fishing lodge at Stump Lake, brings guests for a visit. The visitors are an eclectic group of varied talents, who all have one thing in common: They recognize the solace

> We humans are all rooted in our past. We have lived closely connected to the earth and its creatures. We know a simple truth that is somehow reawakened in nature. There is a distant memory that dances in our souls, in unison with the spirit of the earth. That spirit flows freely, through the hearts of those who leave the confines of their individual identity, for the greater truth of their soul. That soul is one in the community of all life, and knows that oneness in its fondest dreams.

Aspens in the fall

in this beautiful land. They come to reconnect, to revisit their beginnings.

We humans are all rooted in our past. We have lived closely connected to the earth and its creatures. We know a simple truth that is somehow reawakened in nature. There is a distant memory that dances in our souls, in unison with the spirit of the earth. That spirit flows freely, through the hearts of those who leave the confines of their individual identity, for the greater truth of their soul. That soul is one in the community of all life, and knows that oneness in its fondest dreams.

Horses have an ability to break through the barriers that keep us separate. They push our parameters and stoke the fires of our fears, until they blaze fiercely, and exhaust their fuel, leaving behind the ashes of their passion.

There in the afterglow is quiet reflection and inspiration. Like a phoenix rising, we draw power from the flames, and drifting skyward, breathe in the atmosphere of lightness and of love. Beyond our earthly confines, we remember who we are.

We are all one and the same.

EPILOGUE

I remember a time in my horse relationships when I thought it safer to bail out in an emergency. This was a time before I trusted the connection. I feared the power of the horse, and inevitably, the horse knew it.

The moment they acted out my fearful scenario, I leapt off, usually to my detriment. I remember a moment after years of this behavior, wanting to take the leap, but still afraid to, that I had a revelation. I think it was after reading The Tao of Equus that I fully understood the magnitude of my misplaced beliefs. Horses mirror our thoughts and our emotions. Simple.

I was riding in the hills on Prima, then a three-year-old, and the two other riders I was with were hesitant, to say the least. All three horses spooked at a herd of cows sneaking up the hill, and my two other companions leapt off, leaving Diva and Luxy to gallop home. When they passed Prima, who was only in a halter, I knew it would be very painful for me not to ride this out.

Off I went, galloping with the others. It reminded me of the first time I had fully embraced the roller coaster. Instead of dying of a heart attack, I found it joyful, exhilarating. It is all in your perspective. I threw myself into the uncontrolled gallop of my horse. I was one with her, and we three ran uphill and downhill and around corners, completely out of control, to come to a grinding halt at

"Cattle Company" — painting by the author

the paddock fence. I was one of the horses.

It was a huge breakthrough—love and freedom, as opposed to limitation and fear.

That was the beginning of my understanding. There are so many perspectives in horse training. I, however, gravitate toward the ones that speak of partnership, or harmony, or centeredness.

There is an elusive connection, a bond that transcends our current belief systems. Horses can be ridden without tack. They can be approached through fun and in the spirit of play. The Zen moment is when they and we forget ourselves and become joined in the spirit of truth and dance.

The truth is, it is all okay, no need for fear. Become harmless and you are not harmed. There is a place that we can reach in our understanding where life is a dream, our dream, and the horse can take us there. They carry us beyond fear to a place where we are always safe, in our home together.

Animals can teach us the path to spirit because they live there, and if we allow them to contribute to the conversation, they will invite us to experience the ultimate communion in being one with the herd.

Another spring turns to summer on Gateway. Five perfect new babies are running with the herd, each unique and special, and all very loved. My two little pintos are quite the colorful addition. L.E. is so proud, and more protective than usual of Crystal Edition, having lost her baby last year.

It is mid-July and the grass is still green. I wake early this morning to a beautiful sunrise, descend to the kitchen, and go straight to my window. Outside there are four young horses at the hay feeder, which means that the "mamas" have taken over the barn. I sneak along the hallway in my slippers and down the ladder. Rhythmic breathing and gentle snores permeate the air below, and spread evenly across the deep sawdust is the rest of my herd. I pick my way between bodies, not wanting to wake them, and I sit in the morning sun by the large front door.

"Into the Hills" — painting by the author

This is meditation at its finest. Peace and joy are more present here than in any place of worship, and I'm overflowing with the experience. There is a rightness in my world and it is here and now among these peaceful creatures. They fill my days with meaning and new understanding, and worship in this religion of HORSE illumines my life. I have found the truth by immersion, to the point where the boundary of self is no longer distinct, and all that remains is the congregation and community of spirit.

I have earned my way to a privileged place in the herd, where I ask nothing, and consequently am given all.

We have come a long way my friend, through uncertainty, confusion, misinterpretation;
carried by the wings of love to a far greater understanding than we could have ever
believed.

Imagine a world where all minds are joined in the quest for greater understanding.
You and I can change the world, one mind at a time.

Imagine!

—Premiere Edition (Prima)